COVER LETTERS

They Don't Forget

COVER LETTERS

They Don't Forget

Eric R. Martin
Karyn E. Langhorne

Printed on recyclable paper

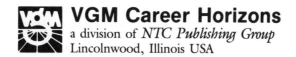 **VGM Career Horizons**
a division of *NTC Publishing Group*
Lincolnwood, Illinois USA

Library of Congress Cataloging-in-Publication Data

Martin, Eric R.
   Cover letters they don't forget / by Eric R. Martin & Karyn E.
Langhorne.
      p.   cm.
  ISBN 0-8442-4139-3
  1. Cover letters. 2. Job hunting.   I. Langhorne, Karyn E.
II. Title. III. Series.
HF5383.M29 1993
808′.0665—dc20

           92-38541
             CIP

1994 Printing

Published by VGM Career Horizons, a division of NTC Publishing Group.
© 1993 by NTC Publishing Group, 4255 West Touhy Avenue,
Lincolnwood (Chicago), Illinois 60646-1975 U.S.A.
3 4 5 6 7 8 9 0 VP 9 8 7 6 5 4 3 2

Contents

About the Authors

Eric Martin is a free-lance writer and a full-time MBA student at the University of Georgia. His major concentrations and research at the university are focused on strategic management of human resources and recent corporate staffing issues. Eric plans to work in human resources consulting upon graduation in June of 1993 and to continue writing books on current work-force trends.

Prior to enrolling in graduate school, Eric worked directly under a well-known management consultant and college professor in Atlanta whose corporate training program added to the development of the concepts in this book. Eric's work experience also includes two years of accounting after earning his undergraduate degree from the Emory University School of Business Administration in 1990.

Eric was born and raised in the suburbs of New York City and now resides with his family in Roswell, Georgia.

Karyn E. Langhorne is an attorney and graduate of the Harvard Law School. After practicing labor law with an Atlanta law firm for two years, Ms. Langhorne initiated a work-at-home legal research business, preparing legal memorandum on a free-lance basis for a number of corporate clients. During that period, she also began her career as a free-lance writer, teaming up with coauthor Eric R. Martin to write this book. Her legal publications include *Missouri Debt Collections* (1992 supplement), published by the Harrison Book Company, and a 1992 update of volume 3 of the *Encylopedia of Georgia Law,* also published by the Harrison Company. She is also currently working on a novel entitled *Indigo Blues.*

Ms. Langhorne is currently a legal editor for a major trade association and resides in Washington, D.C.

PART ONE

Introduction: What You Need to Know

Why You Need This Book

The Old Stuff Doesn't Work

You are the personnel director of the Acme Company. Your company will hire four management trainees this fall, but you have received over 300 resumes and letters of inquiry. Most of the cover letters read like this:

P.O. Box 4805
Citytown University
Citytown, USA 12345

Ms. Ann Jones
Recruiting Director
Acme Company
800 South Main Street
Citytown, USA 12345

Dear Ms. Jones:

I am writing to you to be considered for the management trainee position with your company.

I graduated from Citytown University in June with a major in business administration. As a part of my major, I interned with Apex Company last summer, serving in a variety of corporate capacities. Additionally, in college, I was president of Citytown University's chapter of Young Professionals. In this capacity, I managed our on-campus business, a snack bar called Eats. I am a fast learner and believe that I would be an asset to your firm.

Enclosed please find my complete resume. References will be made available to you on request.

I look forward to hearing from you.

Sincerely,

Jane Doe

Now consider the following letter.

P.O. Box 4805
Citytown University
Citytown, USA 12345

Ms. Ann Jones
Recruiting Director
The Acme Company
800 South Main Street
Citytown, USA 12345

Dear Ms. Jones:

As a result of Acme Company's recent acquisition of Foodstuff International, employees with knowledge of restaurant management and food service would be a particular asset to your company. My experiences managing a snack shop, my degree in business administration, and my internship with Apex Company make me an ideal candidate for Acme's management trainee program.

At Citytown University, I served as president of the Young Professional's club. I was responsible for Eats, a snack bar which catered to college students. Under my direction, Eats initiated a coupon book and a daily specials program which increased the restaurant's profitability by 15 percent.

Through my internship with Apex, I was exposed to other aspects of business, including Apex's new computerized data access system. I believe that the skills I developed during my internship would transfer easily to Acme. Furthermore, these experiences illustrate my ability to quickly master new concepts and assume complex responsibilities.

My resume is included with this letter, but I will contact you next week to answer any questions you may have about me or my background.

I look forward to talking with you about myself, Eats, and how I can become a part of the Acme Company.

Sincerely,

Jane Doe

Which letter do you like better? The same basic information is included in both efforts, but the second letter tells you more. It includes more details, both about the seeker's experiences and her identity as a person. It conveys ability, confidence, leadership, and ambition, without using any of those words.

This is the kind of letter we want to teach you to write. Our basic premise is this: the standard resume and cover letter that saturated the market in the 1980s is obsolete in today's employment world.

Employers, personnel directors, and recruiting coordinators remember letters that express more than just the facts (I have a degree and I want this job) but that also communicate something of who you are and why you would be the perfect addition to their company. A creative letter will leave the reader with the feeling that this is a person he or she would like to meet—and get you a call requesting your presence at an interview. It's not enough for you to copy a form letter out of a book.

Are you ready to learn how to write the cover letter that works? Read on.

2

Why the 1990s Are Different

A Brief History Lesson

We know. You didn't pick up this book to get a history lesson. But the fact of the matter is this: even in job hunting, those who do not know the mistakes of the past are doomed to repeat them. So resist the temptation to skip to more interesting sections of the book, and read this section. Learn how your moment in employment time is different from previous ones and how to address those differences effectively.

From Workers to Employees

Since the turn of the century, every decade of workers has had a particular character. In the twenties, for example, mass production and the growth of the factory resulted in labor unions. For the employees of that era, more than in any generation before or since, a movement to change the operation of factories to protect workers' rights was particularly important.

The worker of the 1930s, however, had different needs. You may remember from your history classes that government work programs characterized that era. Because so many men and women were deeply and harshly affected by the Great Depression, federal projects were initiated to put people back to work. Among those efforts were the Works Program Administration (WPA) and the Civilian Conservation Corps (CCC).

World War II sent women into the work force in record numbers in the forties—you've probably heard about Rosie the Riveter and Wilma the Welder. But by the fifties, Mom was back at home while Dad went off to work. The fifties generation embraced the notion of the *company man,* who, once hired, worked his way up the ranks to retire after thirty years with a pension and a gold watch. Promotions were based on both seniority and merit. Somewhere in that time, the term *worker* gave way to *employee.*

From Social Consciousness to Yuppies

By contrast, the individualism of the 1960s is well documented. That generation's work force is associated with equal rights and social changes. Not suprisingly, careers accenting social awareness experienced a growth surge then. In 1960, the Peace Corps was created, and by 1966, there were over 15,000 Peace Corps members operating in 55 countries.

Inflation and shortages returned us to more traditional employment in the seventies, as a new generation recognized that it might have to sacrifice individual drive for a secure paycheck. And by the 1980s, an upswing in economic growth and an explosion in information technology labelled a generation of new employees: *yuppies* (young upwardly mobile persons). You remember them—the same folks who made *BMW, investment banking,* and *stress* household words.

A Melting Pot of Attitudes

Although the 1990s decade is still in its infancy, *yuppie* is already considered a four-letter word (even yuppies themselves are quick to disclaim it). This generation of employees has its own attitude about itself and its work that encompasses elements of all the attitudes of those who came before: security is important, but so is flexibility. The values of success in the large corporate framework are not dismissed, but individualism and social consciousness are also reaching new zeniths. While materialism is still the American way, the 1990s are already teaching us the harsh lessons that result from living above one's means. So far, the 1990s are proving to be more practical, less excessive, and much more competitive than previous decades.

In other words, the nineties are a melting pot of attitudes—sort of a gumbo of ingredients—that give this difficult decade it own character. And in order to compete in the nineties job market, the first task is to figure out who this generation of job hunters is and what its prospective employers will expect of them.

Table 2.1

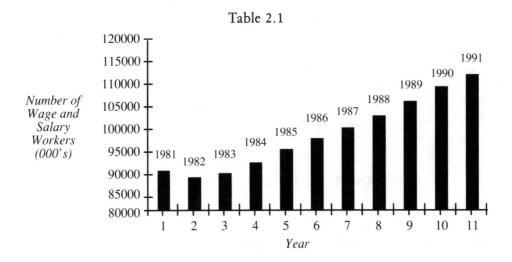

Table 2.2

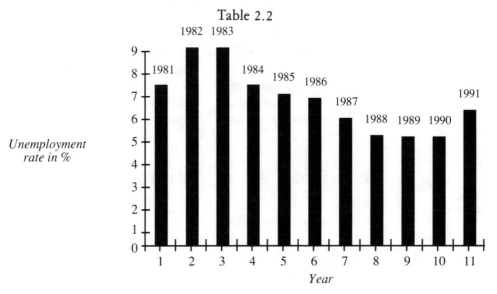

How the 1990s Are Different: Thinking about the Facts

Fewer Jobs

Federal employment studies indicate a decline in the growth of the civilian labor force (excludes military and self-employed persons), as shown in table 2.1. This trend is predicted to continue throughout the decade, creating fewer new jobs each year. The good news is, however, that if you know how to use this information to your advantage, you will increase your chances of getting an interview.

After a drop in the unemployment rate in the mid-eighties due to the upswing of the economy, that figure is already back on the rise in the first two years of the 1990s. If you recall, employers in the 1980s were hiring as many competent individuals as their budget would allow. Today, however, there are not only fewer jobs available, there are more qualified people looking to fill those positions. You should begin to see how standing out in a crowd of qualified applicants is more important now than ever.

It's just a fact that employers are hiring fewer new employees. In fact, new hires at most fortune 500 corporations had dropped to 1 percent of the total work force. A Michigan State University Career Development and Placement Services study estimated that the number of entry-level positions declined by 13.3 percent in 1991. And while few new employees are being hired, bankruptcies are at an all-time high. According to recent surveys, more businesses failed in 1990 than at any time prior to 1983. That number has continued to rise.

More Workers

But while it appears that the hiring boom of the 1980s is receding, there appears to be no significant decrease in college enrollment. In fact, some colleges and universities are reporting that, because of the scarcity of jobs in the nineties, those who didn't finish their undergraduate work are returning to complete their degree. And college grads are enrolling in graduate programs in record numbers, hoping that extra education will give them the competitive edge.

Standing Out in a Crowd

As you can see, there is a trend here. And what it boils down to is simply this: there are more qualified applicants out there and fewer jobs to get. Tough as job hunting is in the best of times, for the nineties job seeker, things are even tougher. In order to distinguish yourself, you must somehow set yourself apart from the crowd. The aim of this book is to help you to use your cover letter to do just that. The resume highlights your qualifications and experiences. If done correctly, a standard resume is an efficient way to communicate your past experiences. Let's keep it that way. The cover letter, however, expresses more than your qualifications. It says something about your goals, potential as an employee, motivation, and style—all of which make your application unique and worth the time to call for an interview. Use the cover letter to your advantage: learn how to catch the reader's eye so that he or she wants to learn more.

The Attitude of the 1990s: Who Is Your Generation?

Before getting into the specifics of cover letters, take a moment to read about the other trends in the 1990s. One of these may be of particular interest to you and your job search. A quick rundown of the events and concerns of the past few years indicates that 1990 employees have a markedly different attitude toward work from their 1980 counterparts. A survey of college freshmen conducted by the University of California Graduate School of Education and the American Council on Education revealed that 1990s students have attitudes more similar to their 1960s counterparts. Thirty-seven percent more of these students have participated in a demonstration (a higher percentage than any since they started doing their survey in 1966). But at the same time, 75 percent admitted that they hope to be well off financially and are attending college to achieve that aim. All of this means that there is yet another shift in what is important in the world of work, and we can expect to see some changes as employers respond to new ideals.

What do employers want from the 1990s? The same thing employers have always wanted: more productivity (whatever goods or services that may be) at less cost (salaries, raw materials, etc.), resulting in increased profits and growth. Of course, that's very simplified, but it's something to always keep in mind when looking for a job. Remember that any job search is a matter of selling a company something—namely, yourself. Your mission, should you choose to accept it, is to convince your target that you are exactly what it needs to increase its profitability—even if it doesn't know it needs you yet.

Now that your have some idea of the lay of the land of this decade, let's focus our attention on what shoes we need to wear to travel on it.

PART TWO

To Thine Own Self Be True: Creativity and Self-Expression

Creativity—the Key to Standing out in the Crowd

Putting your own personality into your letters is vital to the success of your job search, but, of course, there are limits. You wouldn't want to send a cover letter on purple stationery dotted with gold spangles—even if you consider purple your signature color! Red ink isn't such a good idea, either. You get the point. But within the constraints of the business world, there is more room than you think both to express yourself and catch a prospective employer's eye.

Before you can write a cover letter that expresses your personal style, character, and abilities, you have to know them yourself. Some of you may feel this section is unnecessary; however, you will find it helpful in order to fully understand how different letter styles have been categorized in the following chapters. For those who would like to learn what key words and phrases best describe you, this section offers you four lists of words and phrases describing different personal styles. These will, undoubtedly, help you accurately describe your personal qualities and how you can relate these qualities to your past experiences for maximum cover letter effect.

You will also do some exercises that will help you determine what personal attributes prospective employers in your field are looking for as well as the basic research tools for gathering information about companies to which you plan to send a cover letter.

When you can more accurately describe your personal strengths, have a better understanding of what an employer is looking for, and have researched the company, you will be ready to begin constructing the actual cover letter. For now, concentrate on learning more about yourself and your future employer.

3

The First Step to Creativity: Who Am I?

Behavioral studies have shown that 80 percent of a person's success is due to personal qualities rather than experience. Although technical skills are necessary to get the job done, they are less important than basic personality issues to overall success. A person can be trained to handle particular tasks, but personal characteristics rarely change.

Behavioral research also suggests that the most effective people are those who understand themselves. By recognizing your strengths and weaknesses, you can develop strategies to meet the demands of your environment. By understanding your own personal style, you will be able to express yourself more clearly, both in writing and verbally.

In your cover letter, expressing your true strengths, interests, and personal style will get you interviews for jobs in which you would be most successful and satisfied. In fact, research suggests that over half of the people in the western world are in the wrong job. Why? Because their personal style conflicts with their job responsibilities. To avoid this kind of mistake, you must first know yourself and understand the kinds of positions which match your style.

In the past, employers placed too much emphasis on education, skills, and training and, consequently, hired the wrong people for the job. Today, however, employers are assessing and emphasizing job compatibility as well as an applicant's potential to learn the skills necessary to successfully fill the available position. The cover letter is the first, and may be the only, chance you have to show an employer that you have those qualities. When you can demonstrate that you may be what the employer is looking for in your letter, you get invited to the next level—the interview.

13

In the cover letter, it's easy to say (and everyone does) that you will be an asset to the organization. But a prospective employer wants to know *how*. Your qualifications and work experience (that is, your resume) show that you may be able to handle a job and that you have potential as a good employee. Someone who is an asset to an organization, however, has more than good qualifications. An asset to a bookkeeping department, for example, may be someone who majored in accounting, is cautious, and emphasizes an attention to detail. An executive property manager who is an asset, however, majored in business and places less emphasis on detail and more on doing whatever it takes to get the job done on time. In the letter, say you are qualified, but also say how and why you are qualified.

In this chapter, you will learn more about yourself and about what you should convey to prospective employers in your cover letter. You will also learn about the kinds of positions in which you would most likely be compatible. This is only a guideline to help you determine what you should say in your letter and where you would probably have the most success in getting an interview. When you have a better understanding of your personal strengths and qualifications, you will be able to determine, on your own, what you can say that will catch the attention of prospective employers and ultimately lead to an interview.

Analyzing Your Style: How Do You Do Things?

This section will help you choose the proper kinds of describing words to use in your cover letters based on a simple evaluation of your personal style. Before we move on to the evaluation, however, let's consider the following example cover letter to show you how personal style affects your writing.

Evaluating Personal Style

Andrea Lowenstein is an MBA student with several years of direct marketing experience. Andrea has returned to school so that she can move into the field of corporate communication and shareholder relations. Based on her evaluation (which you will do for yourself later in the chapter), Andrea has pulled out of the lists provided these key words and phrases:

Initiated	Persuaded
Self-starter	Interacted well
Reached set goals	Confident about

Now consider this first draft of Andrea's cover letter.

Dear Vice President, Shareholder Relations:

I am writing to you concerning a position in your corporate communications and shareholder relations department. I am currently an MBA student at the Smooze Business School in Atlanta, Georgia.

During my first year, I participated in the Smooze Business School Marketing Association and was a research assistant for my communications professor. I am focusing my course work in the areas of communication strategy and business marketing. With my degree, I believe I could handle the responsibilities in your shareholder relations department.

Before returning to graduate school, I graduated from Country Club University with a BBA in marketing. My full-time work experience includes almost two years of direct marketing with ABC, Inc., where I was responsible for over 80 accounts and $2 million in advertising sales.

I believe my education and skills have prepared me for a position with your company and would appreciate the opportunity to meet with you. I will call you next week to discuss arranging an interview. Thank you for your time.

What do you think? This letter is not too bad. Andrea gets to the point and asks for an interview. But have you noticed how often she starts her sentences with *I*? This letter is typical of most that pass through the hands of prospective employers. The reader sees only one thing—me, me, me. There's nothing about this letter that makes Andrea stand out, and we know nothing about her individual strengths. With just a little help, a few important buzz words, and some research on the company (which will be discussed later in the chapter), her letter could have been much more interesting, creative, informative, and, most importantly, remembered. Now consider Andrea's letter using the phrases and words she pulled out of our lists:

Dear Vice President, Shareholder Relations:

In order to successfully implement a total quality management strategy, your company must continually transfer information to everyone from the CEO and shareholders to the employees of regional distributors. With my marketing experience and future MBA from the Smooze Business School, I am **confident** that I could help convey this information and become a valuable addition to your corporate communications department.

As an MBA student at the Smooze Business School, I have enhanced my communication skills while working as a graduate assistant to the senior lecturer in communication strategy. Additionally, I recently **initiated** production of a brochure soliciting over fifty companies to participate in the Smooze Business School Marketing Association competition for the best marketing plan. We have already **reached our goals** by **persuading** 12 companies to work with our students over the next several months.

Before returning to graduate school, I spent two years in marketing and advertising. In that time, I further developed my communication skills by **working closely with** and presenting proposals to over 80 distribution centers and stores. I believe these skills can directly transfer to your corporate communications department.

I am interested in working with ABC, Inc., upon graduation next May and would appreciate the opportunity to further discuss how my skills and goals match your needs. I will call you next week to discuss arranging a meeting. Thank you for your consideration.

Now what do you think? By incorporating just a few key phrases and words into your cover letter, you are almost forced to think of better, more descriptive ways to say the simple ''I have this degree, and I need a job.'' This letter conveys not only that Andrea has some good experience and an MBA but that she is also someone who gets things started, who reaches goals and who can work well with clients and co-workers. If these letters came from two different people, whom would you choose to interview: The ''I'' person with the degree or the one who gets things done, works well with others, and has an MBA? The choice is obvious.

Evaluating Your Own Style

Now let's move on to the evaluation of your own personal style. This next section will help you determine which key phrases and words you may wish to add to your cover letter.

Our evaluation is based on the best known and most widely accepted approach to understanding behavior and is based on the work of Dr. William Moulton Marsten, who classified behavioral responses into four styles: dominance, inducement, submission, and compliance. Later work by Bill Bonstetter of T.T.I. Software, Ltd., identified the styles as dominant (High D), influencing (High I), steady (High S), and cautious (High C). We have adopted Mr. Bonstetter's terminology to maintain consistency throughout the rest of the book when discussing different letter styles.

Each person is a combination of these four behavioral styles, creating a personality pattern. Is this 100 percent true? Yes, no, and maybe. You will determine which set of words and phrases best describes you based on a list of words for each style. After you determine which list or lists best describes you, check with a friend or collegue who knows you well enough to affirm the accuracy of the adjectives you feel may not be characteristic of your style. By understanding your own style, you will be able to convey your innate strengths in your cover letter, which otherwise go unstated in your resume.

As you complete this section, we will show you the techniques to incorporate each personal style into a cover letter. Most of you, however, will find some adjectives in two or three columns that describe you accurately. In appendix A at the end of this book, there are several examples of cover letters that incorporate these combinations of different styles.

Getting Started

The following lists describe words for each personal style: High D, High I, High S, and High C. Choose the column or columns that best describe you or that most accurately state how you might describe your characteristics in a cover letter. If you find that each column describes something about you, then choose only the two that describe you best. From now on, when we discuss different styles of letters, we will refer to the writers or letters themselves as the High D, I, S, or C or some combination. This simply means that the person writing the letter used key words and phrases that would fit under one of the following categories:

HIGH D	HIGH I	HIGH S	HIGH C
Initiate	Persuade	Assist	Work independently
Invent	Convince	Help	Cooperate with
Persist	Admired by	Devoted	Receptive to
Dare to	Charm	Loyal	Work well with others
Compete with	Excited about	Remain calm	Precise
Determined	Interact well	Considerate of	Accurate
Unafraid to	Inspired by	Patient	Open to suggestion
Independent	Motivate others	Spend long hours	Attention to detail
Self-starter	Personable	Moderate	Firm's moderator
Risk	Well-spoken	Control	Double check
Challenge	Outgoing	Get along with	Gatekeeper
Assertive	Confident	Willing	Well-disciplined
Refuse to quit	Deserve	Collaborate with	Hard worker
Explore	Optimistic about	Accomodate	Respected by others
Pioneer	Enjoy group activities	Trusted by others	Good natured
Speak freely about	Easy to work with	Complete assignments	Extremely organized
Direct	Enthusiastic about	Listen well	Quality oriented
Decisive	Confident about	Traditional hard	Meet high standards
Sense of urgency	People oriented	worker	Seek correctness
Results oriented	Influence	Hold trade secrets	Analytical
Look at bottom line	Manage well	Loyal to company	Conservative
Good under pressure	Opportunity to	Establish relationships	Anticipate problems

HIGH D	**HIGH I**	**HIGH S**	**HIGH C**
Get the job done	Increase sales	Complete repetitive tasks	Structured job
Set priorities	Liked by others	Teamwork oriented	Perfectionist
Reach set goals	Called upon to speak	Systematic procedures	Define expectations
Work fast	Client relations	Dependable	Logically solve
Enjoy challenges	Spoke highly of	Professional attitude	Always prepared
Accept freedom	Lead team projects	Diligent worker	Comply with rules
Work well under pressure	Confided in	Finish work on time	Consistent performer
		Sincere	

A Review of Your Style

After you have reviewed each of the four styles and discussed your results with others, make notes of your choices of the best describing words and phrases in the spaces provided. Of course, these lists are not exclusive, so add your own personal phrases and words based on any style patterns you may have uncovered.

Most prominent D-style phrases (if any):

_____   _____

_____   _____

_____   _____

_____   _____

_____   _____

Most prominent I-style phrases (if any):

_____   _____

_____   _____

_____   _____

_____   _____

_____   _____

Most prominent S-style phrases (if any):

_____   _____

_____   _____

_____   _____

_____   _____

Most prominent C-style phrases (if any):

_____   _____

_____   _____

_____   _____

_____   _____

The Relationship: Cover Letter and Personal Style

Think about your past leadership and work experiences; now is a good time to look at your resume. How can you relate your personal style to your accomplishments? For example, if you won an accounting award in college, you may say that you earned the award because you are the type of person who values correctness and has a need to get the job done to perfection. Can you see how this will help create a cover letter that gets the attention of the reader? Not only does this convey that you won an accounting award, which should already be carefully positioned on your resume, it says something about yourself and how you will perform, which is not stated anywhere on the resume. Before you connect these key phrases and words to your past experiences, consider the following examples.

An advertisement for the following position in your local paper reads:

Bold, growing organization seeks tal-
ented individual to train for challenging
job managing grass-roots issues and election campaigns. Excellent communication and people skills a must. Experience
with political campaigns, commitment to
environmental concerns a plus.

Assume for the purposes of this exercise that four people—a High D, High
I, High C, and High S—all submit letters and resumes for the job. Let's also
pretend that their resumes are substantially the same; all have worked with a
campaign to encourage recycling on their college campus, and all will graduate
with a degree in political science.

Despite each job applicant's similarities, using the D-I-S-C personality style
lists results in unique and energetic letters for each person that clearly point to
individual personal strengths. On the next several pages are four letters—one for
each personality style—that won't be forgotten. In each letter, the D-I-S-C words
and phrases apear in bold type.

High D Cover Letter

Dear Sir or Madam:

Even though recycling is now a habit for millions of Americans, before my administration as student body president, Citytown College had no campuswide recycling effort. In our computer lab alone, thousands of sheets of paper were wasted unnecessarily.

While student body president, I **initiated** a plan to install paper recycling bins in the lab and receptacles for aluminum cans in the snack bar and **challenged** my fellow students to make changes in their habits. Beginning with a series of flyers placed in student mailboxes, followed by discussion groups in which this and other environmental concerns were explored, I galvanized a movement to make recycling a part of our campus tradition. Despite some resistance to the idea from the school's administration, I **persisted,** culminating the effort with a sit-in in front of the president's office. We **achieved our goal:** Citytown College now recycles.

I believe my college experiences illustrate that I **enjoy challenges** and possess the **independence** and **resourcefulness** to be highly effective with your organization.

I hope you will consider me.

High I Cover Letter

Dear Prospective Employer:

In classes for my major, political science, the basic tactics of any grass-roots organizations were thoroughly discussed: direct mailings, door-to-door canvassing, strategic placements of signs and posters to galvanize supporters and volunteers. Through my experiences with student government, however, I have successfully put these tools to work to **persuade** my fellow students, faculty, and administration of Anytown University to implement a recycling program.

I had the **opportunity** to **lead a team** of ten students who were concerned when we realized that our campus did not recycle. **Together, we** developed a strategy to **motivate our community** through rallies, speeches, and buttons. We strove to **enlighten** people about a number of environmental issues. Within a few weeks, the entire school was **excited and involved** in the effort. At last, **I won an audience** with the president of Anytown University and **encouraged him** to consider our proposals. Today, the university has an active recycling program, and many individuals have changed their habits to become more environmentally aware.

I think this experience, as well as my resume, illustrates that I am an **outgoing, people-oriented idividual who interacts well** with others, and that I could be a valuable asset to an organization like yours. Please consider me for this position.

High S Cover Letter

Dear Sir or Madam:

Professionals who demonstrate the ability to **work hard, get along well with others, listen,** and **complete complex assignments** in a **timely** and **dependable** manner are assets to any political organization. These are abilities I have developed through my work with the student government at Maintown State, which I could offer your organization.

As a political science major with a **sincere** interest in environmental issues affecting our society, I **collaborated with** other concerned students to **develop a plan** to make recycling a campuswide priority. I **spent long hours** on this initiative and **was involved in all stages** of the effort: from brainstorming on slogans to painting posters, from outlining the issues to be presented to distributing flyers. The experience taught me a great deal about **the value of teamwork in achieving common goals.**

I believe I have much to contribute to your organization and hope you will contact me for an interview.

High C Cover Letter

Dear Reader:

Organization is the key to a successful grass-roots effort. In my efforts to bring recycling to Normal University, I managed a campuswide team of volunteers through a careful and **detailed** plan that achieved our goal.

In **cooperation with** the faculty and the administration, I **analyzed** how recycling could best be implemented on our campus and developed a plan that could both reduce waste and be easily integrated in our community. Today at Normal University, receptacles for bottles, cans, and paper are strategically located throughout the grounds. In addition, I **organized** a series of lectures on several environmental issues that have been well recieved by students and faculty alike.

As a **hard worker** and a **careful planner** who has demonstrated **solid people skills** and the **ability to coordinate** a campaign, I believe my skills could be well used within your organization. I hope to discuss them with you in an interview soon.

As you can see, whatever your personal style, the D-I-S-C words and phrases give your reader information about your character and skills. While these letters try to convey dominant personality styles, as we discussed earlier, everyone has elements of each style—D, I, S, and C. Consequently, you can write a letter that has both I and C phrases or D and S or any other combination. Examples of letters that mix personal styles are included in appendix A of this book.

In addition to the use of the highlighted words and phrases, you may have noticed other similarities in these letters. Each opens with an attention-getting sentence. They don't start with ''I saw this ad in the newspaper.'' They start with something interesting about the job seeker or about the job or even about the world in general, provided it is relevant to the job or to the job seeker's qualifications. The next paragraph elaborates on the facts the writers have chosen to reveal about themselves, giving more details about who they are and why they are something special. Finally, they close their letters by repeating or summarizing. Voila! There is a dynamic cover letter!

Now that you have a better understanding of how to use these lists of words, in the following exercises relate your personal style to as many past experiences as you can. You will probably use each experience in different cover letters, depending on the person to whom you are writing and the kind of position for which you are applying. Don't worry about sentence structure here. That will be discussed later.

Personal style or phrase _____

How does this relate to your past successes and why?

_____

_____

_____

_____

Personal style or phrase _____

How does this relate to your past successes and why?

_____

_____

_____

_____

Personal style or phrase _____

How does this relate to your past successes and why?

_____

_____

_____

_____

Personal style or phrase _____

How does this relate to your past successes and why?

_____

_____

_____

_____

Personal style or phrase _____

How does this relate to your past successes and why?

_____

_____

_____

_____

Before moving on to the actual construction of your cover letter, you must complete two more simple tasks: gathering information to understand what an employer is looking for in an applicant and gathering information on the company itself.

4

The Second Step to Creativity: To Whom Am I Writing?

This section is divided into three parts encompassing everything you need to know about to whom you are writing: the general audience, the prospective employer's point of view, and the facts beyond your personal style.

The General Audience

The audience your letter is to reach determines how creative you can be. You may decide to send a personnel director a more conservative letter than the letter you might send to a CEO, for example. In other circumstances, the reverse might be true. The kind of company or organization you are contacting and the level of the person to whom you are writing affects the way you write. This section proposes the basic research steps that will help you determine how far you can go and still get what you want.

Although it may be impossible to get information about everyone to whom you send a cover letter and resume, there are many circumstances when only one or two pieces of information will be extremely helpful. If you can determine a prospective employer's personal style (High D, I, S, or C), for example, you will

27

be able to construct a letter that matches that personality and keeps the reader's attention. The following are examples of what you may want to focus on in your cover letter based on your audience's personal profiles. By no means is this list all inclusive. Look back to chapter 3 at the personal profile summaries and use different tactics for different letters.

- High D profile: If you direct a letter to this person, it would be beneficial to discuss leadership positions where you had control and responsibility for making quick decisions. You also have more room to prepare a bold and creative letter.

- High I profile: If you are writing to this person, you may want to talk about your persuasive nature and how you were able to move up the ladder (winning a school election, for example) or to increase sales by using these skills. Again, there is plenty of room to take chances and be creative.

- High S profile: If you are writing to this person, mentioning projects you have accomplished that required time-consuming and repetitive tasks would be beneficial. A more conservative letter may be appropriate here.

- High C profile: If you are writing to this person, talk about how your need to do things to perfection earned you your rank in the top 20 percent of your graduating class. Again, a more conservative letter may be appropriate.

Finding Details that Relate

You are probably asking, ''What will I say about myself if my personal profile differs from that of the person to whom I am writing?'' This will happen often. The key is to get the reader to relate to at least one of your past experiences; this way, the reader feels a kind of attachment to you. Focus your letter on who you are, but also convey to the reader something that he or she can relate to. All of us have had to alter our behavior to fit different situations. A High-D profile bank president, for example, most probably counted coins and reconciled accounts in his or her first or second job out of school. These tasks fit the High S and High C profiles more than High D, but in order to ''pay their dues,'' everyone must perform tasks which do not suit their profile. Can you think of some of the tasks you performed that you did not like? These are probably tasks that fit a personal profile other than yours. Don't ignore them in your letter just because you didn't like them. You learn from everything you do, so use all of your experiences to your advantage.

Gathering Information

Now for the difficult part. How do you determine what the person to whom you are sending a letter wants to see in the letter itself? The following is a list of practical suggestions. Again, thses are not all inclusive. Use your own ideas. Be creative.

- If you are referred to a potential employer, ask the person who referred you questions that would give you a better understanding of the employer's profile. For example, "What kind of person is he or she like?"

- If you can meet the person, do so. Make your own judgment. Try campus socials, a career fair, or a friend of a friend.

- Call the person you are planning to write and ask pertinent questions about the job and the company to which you are applying. Make your own judgment.

- If you know anyone in the company or organization to which you are applying, ask for information. People are usually willing to help if they know you are not trying to steal their job.

- If you know only the job title of the person you are writing, think about his or her daily responsibilities. What profile most likely fits his or her daily tasks? Make an educated guess.

- If you cannot contact anyone directly and you are writing to someone of high power, such as a CEO or president, look for publications, including annual reports, magazine articles, newspaper articles, or Who's Who publications, that say something about special achievements. What profile would most likely match that person's particular achievements? Make an educated guess.

You can see how understanding the profile of the person you are writing affects what you say and how creative you can be. Next you will learn about how the employer views potential employees.

The Employer's Point of View

When prospective employers are considering adding someone new to their organization, a question that always arises is "What kind of person will be the most successful in the position?" Immediately, technical background, education, and previous experiences are considered. Assuming, however, that most qualified applicants send presentable cover letters and resumes, the prospective employer must look to other factors to determine who to call in for an interview. What are some of the factors? Well, creativity and personality make us unique, not our degree. So use those unique characteristics that you believe are applicable (based on the prospective employer's view) to get the interview. Make prospective employers see beyond your degree. Make them see who you are and why you are perfect for their organization.

The cover letter is the only place you will be able to accomplish this unless, of course, the company has the time to interview every qualified candidate who sends in a resume. (Don't worry, there are no companies willing to spend the time or money to do this.) Use your cover letter. Say in it that you are qualified, but also say something about yourself that matches the prospective employer's idea of the perfect candidate.

You're probably asking, "How do you know what an employer wants?" That's easy, once you understand the kinds of positions in which you would most likely succeed. If you have completed all of the previous exercises, you should already have a good idea. Once you have determined that your goals, skills, and style match a particular job, the probability is high that the prospective employer hiring for that job is looking for someone just like you.

Table 4.1 examines what employers look for in potential employees who match certain personal profiles. For example, consider the employer who is looking for someone with a relatively High-I profile. Of course the company recruiter would not say he or she was looking for a High I but instead would describe the qualified candidate as someone who is persuasive, personable, and a good salesperson. Candidates who are involved in many social interactions, have a high trust level, optimistic outlook, skillful use of vocabulary, and a persuasive nature would be preferred. You can see these phrases on the chart at the top near the heading "I."

Another example would be a company looking for someone with a Low D profile. Candidates who prefer consistency and procedures over change, pay attention to deadlines, and have experience doing specialized work activities would most likely be hired. By examining your personal profile and the potential employer's profile, you can focus on, in you cover letter, the kinds of responsibilities you are capable of handling that match the kinds of responsibilities the employer is looking for. You can see the value of table 4.1 now.

You have been reading a lot about the most subjective matters—personal style and employer profiles. This is because all the standard information goes in your resume. Your work experience is related to your personal profile in the cover letter. We assume you already have a resume prepared and that you are trying to determine how you are going to write a cover letter that makes you stand out. The cover letter, remember, describes more than your qualifications. It says something about you and about how you are perfect for the job. However, there is an important area where profiles and resumes are not enough to get an interview. You will learn about this area in the next section.

The Facts Beyond Personal Style

In addition to showing the prospective employer who you are, you must show that you have carefully selected the employer's organization. How? By saying something intelligent about the company, organization, or industry that is either particularly interesting for the reader or relevant to your application. Yes, this involves outside research, but in this section you will learn about several helpful research tools that should get you started.

If you can, you should always say something about the company, firm, or organization to which you are sending a letter in the opening sentence. Of course, this is impossible if you are responding to a blind ad in the newspaper. You will also want to relate what you say about the company to your own experiences

Table 4.1: The Employer's View

D	I	S	C
Complete authority	Many social interactions	Patience & persistence	Precise procedures
Sense of urgency	High trust level	Concentration/one task	High quality
Immediate results	Optimistic outlook	Responsibility	Accurate/systematic
Quick/firm decisions	Skillful use of	Minimal change	Critical analysis
Fast response	vocabulary	Conservative methods	Done right the first time
Directive leadership	Persuasive communicator	Work w/others to	Established rules &
Freedom from outline	Quickly adapt to activity	achieve results	regulations
Creative thinking	Project self-confidence	Strong listening skills	Analytical approach
Act w/o precedent	Fast paced		
Persistent approach to	Working w/people vs.	Analysis of outcomes	Responsibility - limited
winning	things	before delegating	authority
Accepting and initiating	Self-starter	Complete follow-through	Tidy, organized
change	Alertness to problems	Working at steady pace	Conservative
Abstract thinking	Variety of work	Following procedures	Calculating
Mobile work environ.	activities	Guarding sensitive info.	Logical thinking
Opportunity to explore	Flexible use of time		Maintain standards
new ideas	Consulting approach		Quality oriented
	with others		Collecting facts/data
Practical solutions	Team environment	Loyal to people in	Critical analysis of new
Facts & data in	Awareness of deadlines	organization	ideas
Open communication	Care in delegating	Prioritizing tasks	Interact with people
Time to react to change	assignments	Logical approach	Planned use of time
Lead by example	Handle some detailed	Analysis of crises to	Example to follow
Working with things	work	prevent reccurance	Good tolerance level for
	Some routine work		conflict
Consistency in	Analytical skills	Testing of rules and	Open communication
procedures	Ability to weigh pros/	procedures	Freedom to act
Reflective approach to	cons	Limited routine work	Support team
work	Example to follow	Work many projects at	Varied activities
Awareness of deadlines	Working alone	the same time	Mobile work
Predictable environ.	Little interaction w/	Ability to take risks	environment
Specialized work act.	people		Quick response to crises/
	Follow established		changes
	system & procedures		

and personal profile. Presenting the facts shows the reader you have done your homework. Relating them to your experiences shows the reader you are qualified and keeps him or her interested. Your personal style adds something more to your letter and, ultimately, makes you stand out in the crowd. And then you may get a call requesting your presence for an interview. In this section, concentrate on how to do research for your letter. At the end of this section, there are worksheets that will help you keep track of the information you have just learned. In the next three sections, you will learn how to put everything you learned in chapters 3 and 4 together to form the end product—your cover letter.

Unless you are acquainted with a friend, relative, alumni of your school, or someone else who can tell you about the company, firm, or organization, you need access to a good public or university library. An excellent source of information can be obtained from the company itself in the annual report or company newsletter. You can usually get the information you need on how to obtain these publications through the marketing department at the company from which you are seeking employment.

For our purposes, we list sources of information that will help you find information about

The name, address, and telephone number of company headquarters
Names of officers
Size of corporate staff
Products and services
Sales
Financial information
Stability and growth
Divisions, subsidiaries, and affiliates
Rank of company among large corporations
Standing of a company in its industry or field
Occupational outlook in general
History of the company
Plans for new products, services, locations, the future plans

Publications for Finding Out about a Company

The following is a list of useful publications for finding out about a company.

"INC's 500 Fastest Growing Privately Owned Smaller Corporations," *INC* (December)

America's Corporate Families

Banks and Branches Data Book

Business Week, "Corporate Scoreboard" (March)

Corporate and Industry Research Reports (CIRR)

Directory of Corporate Affiliations

Directory of U.S. Corporations (formally *Fortune Double 500*)

Dun & Bradstreet, *Million Dollar Directory*

Encyclopedia of Associations, International Organizations

Facts on File Directory of Major Public Corporations

Forbes, annual directory issue, (each April)

Forbes, "Largest Private Companies in the U.S." (each November or December)

Moody's Manuals

National Newspaper Index

New York Times, Wall Street Journal, other large-city newspapers

Occupational Outlook Handbook

Predicasts F&S Index United States

Reference Book of Corporate Managements

Standard & Poor's Industry Surveys

Standard & Poor's Register of Corporations, Directors, and Executives

The Billion Dollar Directory

The Trinet Top 1500 Companies

The Trinet Second 1500 Companies

The Trinet Top 1500 Private Companies

The U.S. Savings and Loan Directory

Thomas's Register of American Manufacturers

Value Line Investment Survey

Ward's Business Directory of U.S. Private and Public Companies

Who's Who publications

Databases and Directories

There are many databases and directories worth looking into. The following is a list of databases and directories that offer helpful information:

ABI/Inform Ondisc

Business Periodicals Index

CD/Corporate

Corporate and Industry Research Reports (CIRR)

Compact Disclosure

Compuserve

D&B software databases

Disclosure Database

Info Trac

IvesText

Lexis/Nexis

Moody's Corporate databases

National Newspaper Index

PTS Databases

Standard & Poor's Register—Corporate

Trade & Industry Index

Trinet U.S. Businesses

Summary

You have just learned about your audience and how it affects what you say and how creative you can be in your cover letter. You also learned about what an employer looks for in the ideal candidate and how you will use this to your advantage. Finally, you learned about different research tools that will prove to the reader that you have done your homework.

On the next pages, complete the four worksheets, which will help you keep track of the information you just learned. Once you get the hang of it, it becomes second nature, and you will probably develop your own system.

Worksheet 1

Company Name _____ Contact Name _____

Facts about the company worth mentioning in cover letter _____

_____

_____

_____

_____

_____

_____

List everything you know about the person to whom you are sending the
letter: personal profile, background, achievements, responsibilities.

_____

_____

_____

_____

_____

_____

_____

List the phrases and words you chose about yourself, and list one or two words or phrases from table 4.1 that would best describe what this company looks for in a job applicant of your calibre.

_____

_____

_____

_____

_____

_____

_____

Based on your responses, how creative, bold, or conservative should this letter be? _____

Worksheet 2

Company Name _____ Contact Name _____

Facts about the company worth mentioning in cover letter _____

_____

_____

_____

_____

_____

_____

List everything you know about the person to whom you are sending the
letter: personal profile, background, achievements, responsibilities.

_____

_____

_____

_____

_____

_____

_____

_____

List the phrases and words you chose about yourself, and list one or two words or phrases from table 4.1 that would best describe what this company looks for in a job applicant of your calibre.

_____

_____

_____

_____

_____

_____

_____

Based on your responses, how creative, bold, or conservative should this letter be? _____

Worksheet 3

Company Name _____ Contact Name _____

Facts about the company worth mentioning in cover letter

_____

_____

_____

_____

_____

_____

List everything you know about the person to whom you are sending the
letter: personal profile, background, achievements, responsibilities.

_____

_____

_____

_____

_____

_____

_____

List the phrases and words you chose about yourself, and list one or two
words or phrases from table 4.1 that would best describe what this company
looks for in a job applicant of your calibre.

_____

_____

_____

_____

_____

_____

_____

Based on your responses, how creative, bold, or conservative should this letter be? _____

Worksheet 4

Company Name _____ Contact Name _____

Facts about the company worth mentioning in cover letter

_____

_____

_____

_____

_____

_____

List everything you know about the person to whom you are sending the
letter: personal profile, background, achievements, responsibilities.

_____

_____

_____

_____

_____

_____

_____

_____

List the phrases and words you chose about yourself, and list one or two
words or phrases from table 4.1 that would best describe what this company
looks for in a job applicant of your calibre.

_____

_____

_____

_____

_____

_____

_____

Based on your responses, how creative, bold, or conservative should this letter be? _____

This should get you started with your first four cover letters. In the next three chapters, you will learn how to combine the information you have uncovered in the previous worksheets with the personal profile information in chapter 3 and your previous experiences.

Let's briefly review what you have done up to this point so that you can see the big picture. In chapter 3, you picked out key words and phrases that best describe your personal style. You then related your style to your previous experiences. This will be used in the part of the cover letter that discusses your qualifications; the personal profile adds a quality to this section that makes your letter unique. In chapter 4, you determined what your audience wants and needs to hear in order to stay interested. You make friends with the reader, so to speak. The facts show your knowledge of their company in the first section of the letter. Understanding the personal profile of the person to whom you are writing will allow you to construct a letter that will allow readers to relate at least one of their experiences to yours. Finally, by understanding what a prospective employer is looking for in an applicant, you will be able to construct a letter that points out that you have these qualities. You would probably agree that this type of letter is much better than saying, "I have a degree, and I want this job."

It's time to move on to the construction of your letter. Good luck!

PART THREE

The Nitty Gritty: Constructing the Cover Letter

The Hook, Line, and Sinker Approach

Now that you have some idea of who you are (your strengths and your style), who they are (details about the company or organization you are contacting), and what you have to offer them (what elements of your resume and background are most readily adaptable to their needs and structure), you are ready to begin to write your letter.

How do you begin?

Capture the reader's attention. Remember, you are selling yourself to this company, pitching yourself like any other commodity available on the open market. In other words, think of your cover letter as a sixty-second commercial to sell yourself to your prospective employer.

You may be wondering about how to be a commercial. What are you supposed to do, write yourself a slogan and tap dance across a sheet of white bond paper? As crazy as it sounds, that is exactly what we are suggesting you do—but the slogan is a simple, eye-catching phrase, and the tap dancing gets done with your words, not your feet.

Stop and think for a second. What are your favorite commercials? What do you like about them? What makes them effective? Are they funny? Musical? Cute? Sentimental? Whatever the product, the best commercials are, if nothing else, memorable. And whatever the product, all commercials have the same basic elements: an eye-catching beginning; an information section that tells the audience something about the product; and a memorable conclusion, or recap. We call this the hook, line, and sinker approach to cover letters that make the final package unforgettable. Each of these elements will be discussed in this section. Examples of various ideas, with guidelines for strong, clear, and vivid language, will be included. You will do several exercises that relate your experiences to this concept, which you will use to develop each section of your cover letter. However, before you start to develop your own hook, line, and sinker, let's talk about the basics of any good cover letter.

5

Paper and Presentation

Paper

You need to start with clean twenty-pound or better bond paper in an attractive professional hue; it doesn't have to be stark white, but it shouldn't be electric pink, either. Although we've heard stories about people who got jobs by sending resumes and letters written on everything from onion skin to toilet paper, we don't recommend you try things like that. The same rule applies to envelopes. We've heard of job seekers who sent their letters in soda pop bottles and by singing telegram and delivered crumpled resumes in plastic waste baskets. Some of them got the job. But on the whole, an approach like that is a tremendous gamble. You can accomplish just as much with a well-written, neat, professional letter sent through the U.S. mail.

Addresses and Greetings

If at all possible, address your letter to the appropriate person by his or her name and title. A letter of inquiry addressed to ''Ms. Janet Mann, Assistant Director of Personnel'' will be much more effective than a letter addressed to ''Personnel Director'' or worse, ''To whom it may concern.'' Furthermore, some companies have personnel directors, others have recruiting coordinators, and some have vice presidents for human resources. A simple phone call to the receptionist at your target company should get you the right name, its correct spelling, and the full title of the person you are contacting. You might also take that opportunity to find out if there is any special notation you can add to the address to get your letter into the hands of the appropriate person as soon as possible (suite, floor, or box number).

Sometimes you will not be able to obtain any information about the individual who will read your letter—like when you answer a blind ad in a newspaper that requests that you send your letter to a post office box. In this case, you have to deal with the sticky issue of how to address the recipient. As we discussed above, "To whom it may concern" does nothing to build a relationship between you and your audience. In a business context, the informal "Hello" or the flippant "Dear Whomever" probably are not your best bets. Although it is popular, we don't recommend you start with "Dear Sir" either. If your reader turns out to be female, nothing will aggravate her more, and in today's work force, you reader is just as likely to be female as male. So how do you address this letter? Here are some ideas we have run accross:

Dear Madam or Sir:
Dear Personnel Director (or whatever the employer's title is):
Dear Gentleperson (or Gentlepeople, as the case may be):

Dear Reader:
Although it's very formal and somewhat awkward, on the whole we think "Dear Madam or Sir" or the employer's title are the safest greetings. Of course, if you know the identity of your reader, you begin with their name.

Form

You have probably heard the expression "Cleanliness is next to godliness." Well, in the employment world you could phrase that as "Neatness is next to competence." A letter written with ragged margins, faint type, or smudgy ink sends with it the message that the writer is an amateur or that he or she is uneducated or that he or she doesn't care about the job. Make sure that your letter meets the standard margins of a business letter (usually an inch all the way around) and that it is legible and clear. Change the ribbon on your computer printer or typewriter frequently to make certain that your letter can be seen. Have your letter laser printed if at all possible. If you don't have access to a laser printer at home or at school, check your local copy center. For between three to five dollars per quarter hour, you can retype your resume and cover letter and laser print for about one dollar per page.

There are many different ideas about the best format for business correspondence (where your address should go, where to place the date). Any of them, provided you are consistent and logical, will work for your cover letter. For source books on basic letter format, see appendix B of this book.

Grammar

Good grammar, correct spelling, and careful proofreading are critical to the success of your letters. Like neatness, mistakes in these areas send a message to your prospective employer about your intelligence, diligence, and sincerity. Don't blow your chances with a typo. Not everyone is good at proofreading. If you know you tend to leave out words when you write and that you don't always notice the missing word when you re-read your letters, have a friend double-check your letter before you send it. Retyping is a nuisance, but it is better to spend a few extra minutes on the redo than an extra month unemployed!

If you don't already have one, buy yourself a copy of Strunk and White's *The Elements of Style*. It is a wonderful guide to grammar and better writing. If you already have a copy, read it and use it.

Length

Throughout this book, we will talk about the "hook, line, and sinker." We'll deal with them as three sections of your letter, and usually we'll break them into three separate paragraphs. The hook is your first paragraph; the line, the second paragraph; and the sinker, the closing paragraph. If you prepare your letter according to that format, you have a three-paragraph letter that probably won't be longer than a single page.

Although the three-paragraph, single-page cover letter is a good rule of thumb, don't get upset if you need five paragraphs and two pages to present yourself. If what you've written in the line needs to be two paragraphs instead of one, use two paragraphs. Clarity should always be the determining factor. Similarly, if you need a second page to write that killer closing, by all means go ahead. As long as your letter remains interesting and cohesive, length is not a significant problem. Just don't ramble. After you have finished this book, you should be better able to judge for yourself when your cover letter is too long and when it is just right.

Now that we have outlined the basics that form the canvas of our letter, it is time to paint.

6

The Hook

The hook is your opening. It is the first impression, the introduction, the smooth gray business suit, or the silver spandex leotard. This is the opening salvo of your commercial about yourself, and the first few words you use will determine if your letter and its attached resume are read or tossed aside.

We are assuming here that you have already made the efforts necessary to create a good first impression. Your letter is addressed to the right person, is written on 20-pound or better bond paper in clear black type. Its crisp exterior has landed on the desk of the person who determines who will be called for an interview. The employer opens the letter, sees his or her name, and reads.

What are you going to say to get your reader to put you in the interview pile instead of in the trash? How are you going to capture his or her interest? How are you different from and better than everyone else who wants this job?

Years ago, there was a perfume commercial that suggested a woman whisper in order to capture a man's attention. Not mumble—whisper—so that he had to lean close to hear what she had to say. Get it? You want your letter to whisper "hire me," and the first few lines of your letter will, in many cases, determine whether you are in the running.

You may be wondering, "How do I do it?" Well, before you write the hook, review your list of key words and phrases discussed in chapter 3 and what the potential employer needs and wants to know discussed in chapter 4. What aspects about yourself are pertinent in applying for this position? What do you know about the company or person you are writing to that might be helpful? Which of those aspects will be your best avenue to attract the attention of your audience? Think about this as you read this section and work on the examples we have prepared. At the end, you will write your own opening statements based on your own experiences.

Example: Hook 1

Suppose you are applying for a position on the adminstrative staff of the undergraduate program of a large university. You find out about it from an advertisement in the *Chronicle of Higher Education,* and you are basically familiar with the school but lack specific details about the job. After visiting the local library, you discover that the university has recently linked all of its operations in a local area network, including a word processing program, a spreadsheet program, an interoffice mail system, and other programs. Furthermore, a recent catalog names the person who currently holds the position, and you make a telephone call to her and are able to ascertain that among her responsibilities are drafting financial reports; projecting the college's budget for the upcoming fiscal year; interacting with the provost, dean of financial affairs, and the chairpersons of each undergraduate department. You have concluded that her personal profile most closely matches someone with a High C profile.

You have a bachelor's degree in accounting and a minor in computer programming. You have helped your parents by managing the books of their small packing and moving business since you were old enough to understand the principles of accounting. You were treasurer of the student council, and it was your responsibility to disperse the student activities budget among the various clubs and organizations seeking funds. You have chosen words and phrases in chapter three from the High C and High D columns.

With that information, write the hook of your cover letter in the space provided. Remember, the purpose of the hook is to capture your reader's attention. You are sending a signal that you are not just another boring job applicant but someone special with an innovative and creative approach. Try it. You will do exercises that use your own experiences once you have mastered the idea of the hook.

_____

_____

_____

_____

_____

Here are some examples of how not to begin a cover letter:

- This letter is in response to your advertisement in the Citytown *Post*.
- I am writing to you to apply for the administrative assistant position.
- I have heard that Citytown University is a fine place to begin a career in education, and so I am applying.

While each of these sentences is satisfactory (the last one is a little strange but not completely unacceptable), they probably will not make the writer standout. If you began with any of these, you may want to rethink your approach. Loosen up! These exercises are for your eyes only. Get a little wild and crazy! You will be suprised at how a little creativity will improve your writing, yet it will still sound professional and businesslike.

Some of the one-liners we came up with were these:

- As an accounting and computer science graduate, my familiarity with **the detailed** matters of finance and technology make me an ideal choice for the administrative assistant position.
- Because Citytown has recently adopted a local area network linking all campus terminals, a basic familiarity with mainframe computing will be an important criterion for new employees. As my resume indicates, I have **worked many hours** with computers as well as **earned** a degree in accounting and have applicable work experience.
- After speaking with Joy Smith regarding her responsibilities as an administrative assistant, I am confident that I have the skills necessary to assume that position.
- Look no further! I have the background and experience necessary to get the job done efficiently and effectively at Citytown University.

Notice that while each of these suggestions is more creative and informative than the simple declaration "I saw the advertisement, and I want the job," each is still within the standard parameters of a business letter. When we say "creative," we don't mean crazy. We mean more individual, more personal, and more effective, since these qualities indicate that you have taken the time to carefully consider your approach. At the same time, you don't want to say everything there is to know about you in the first paragraph. Flirt a little. Indicate that you are someone with some skills (mention qualities based on your choice of key words and phrases, for example) or knowledge that would be valuable (you might introduce some facts about the company here), but they will have to keep reading to find out more. Your hook is like a mystery novel in a way: It opens with the plot twist, then keeps the reader spellbound until the bitter end.

Example: Hook 2

You are applying for a stockbroker trainee position with a big finance firm. You have a degree in finance, were a member of the business fraternity at your college, and paid for most of your education by working at various sales-related jobs. You know that the founder of the company, Otto Moxie, was a self-made man and heard his granddaughter, Lotta Moxie, the current CEO, speak at your college last year. She stated that she believes in her grandfather's values but intends to take them and the company into the twenty-first century. You are convinced she has a High D or High I profile.

Write an opening:

_____

_____

_____

_____

_____

This example lends itself to getting really ambitious and maybe a little corny, and in an exercise, it is okay if you sound a little like Dale Carnegie on caffeine. How about these:

- Ambition, drive, and foresight. These are the qualities that characterize Moxie, Inc., and its employees. As my resume shows, these are qualities I possess and hope to implement as a stockbroker trainee with your company.

- In her speech to Citytown University last year, I heard Ms. Lotta Moxie's comments about the marriage of old-fashioned hard work and space-age technology. As a 1991 finance graduate who has worked her way through school, I feel I am a stockbroker trainee candidate who would meet Moxie, Inc.'s ideals.

See? These examples just beg you to read the next paragraph. They provide just enough information about you to spark a flicker of interest in the reader. "Who is this person?" the reader asks after a good hook. And to find out, your prospective employer can only keep reading about you.

Example: Hook 3

You are a senior computer science and finance major at State Tech. Your father sent you a copy of his *Citywide Banker's Journal* that had an article about how a local bank is currently implementing Zinc Software's new D-base program.

Your father would really like to see you follow in his footsteps, but you prefer working with computers and not with money. You chose key words and phrases from the High D and High C columns.

Here is a chance to kill two birds with one stone by working in the field of your choice, computers, in the industry your father would appreciate, banking.

Write an opening:

_____

_____

_____

_____

_____

Here are two of our lines. The first one focuses solely on experience and information, while the second focuses more on personality and style. You choose the one you like best—both are equally effective.

- The release of Zinc Software Company's innovative database program has generated the need for organizations like yours, that will implement this program, to hire individuals with the most up-to-date training. As a 1993 graduate of State Tech, I have learned the computer language in which Zinc's D-base program is written. With these skills, I could help Metro Bank efficiently transfer your current records and tailor the program to fit your needs as well as maintain your corporate information system.

- Implementing Zinc Software Company's new D-base program requires not only patience and attention to detail by those responsible for downloading the entire system but leadership skills as well. I believe I fit these criteria and could help Metro Bank efficiently implement Zinc's innovative D-base program as well as maintain your corporate information system.

Both openings focus on something the reader is interested in and needs to know. Whether it is your unique skills or your personality—it doesn't matter. The idea is to get the reader to want to learn more. Both can, and both will.

Example: Hook 4

Now let's assume you have an advanced degree and work experience. Consider this situation. You have a master's degree in social psychology and communication. Your work experience includes over one year working with the management consulting firm AceCorp Consulting. You read in the Citytown *Post* that Emerging Communication Technologies, Inc., has been rated as one of *Fortune* magazine's up-and-comer Fortune 500 companies and is expected to become a leader in international communication. You would like to help advance international business. You have chosen key words and phrases from the High I column.

Write an opening:

_____

_____

_____

_____

_____

We came up with these:

- A concise and accurate presentation is only the first step toward convincing international officials to invest in Emerging Communication Technologies, Inc.'s, new satellite. Persuasive arguments that show ECT will benefit those countries without disrupting their cultures will, undoubtedly, position your company as a leader in the field. With a master's degree in social psychology and communication as well as experience in the communications field, I can help successfully market your new satellite.

- It takes a skilled individual to recognize the needs of different cultures. As Emerging Communication Technologies, Inc., positions its new satellite in the international market, it will need to consider each country's cultures as a factor in determining an effective marketing plan. With my ability to interact well with different people as well as my qualifications, I can help ECT successfully choose and develop the best marketing strategy.

Both openings take advantage of current industry information, and the first adds to that qualification while the second adds personal style. Now let's look at a few less conservative openings that work. Keep in mind that it is just as important to consider who your reader is and what he or she would most likely find eye catching as well as effective.

Example: Hook 5

You have always wanted to get into politics. You are still in school, but you know you qualify for the two-year internship program with your U.S. senator, the honorable Richard D. Cobb. You have recently read that he has supported an education bill that has made him unpopular with certain groups in your state, mainly the teachers' union, and may face a challenge in his next bid for reelection. You're a political science major and fit into the High D category of words and phrases.

You are convinced that Senator Cobb is a High I. Your father's partner's brother's friend Jim Smith worked for Senator Cobb.

Write your opening:

_____

_____

_____

_____

Here are our thoughts for the senator:

- In a recent conversation with our mutual friend Jim Smith, he revealed that your two-year internship program requires an exceptional knowledge of public policy and a dedication to public service. I have that knowledge and feel that dedication.

- Ours is a country of choices—not unlike the choices your office faces in determining the candidates for your two-year internship program for college graduates. As a political science major, I am fascinated by the workings of our great American system and believe that I should be your choice.

- Initiative. A simple word. With it, nothing is impossible. Without it, all is lost.

What do you think? Let's look at the first one. Notice that we used the contact. If you have one, by all means, make use of it. However, we suggest that you avoid sentences like "My father's partner's friend Jim Smith suggested I contact you about the internship program."

There are several problems with this statement. The biggest problem is that it sounds like you only do what people tell you to do. The other problem is that it is boring. It tells the reader nothing about why you are interested in or qualified for the position. Instead, use the techniques you have learned about the hook and the contact's name to make your introductory sentences more effective.

Let's move to the second example. Notice that we didn't use any of the information we provided. We thought that any references to the senator's troubles with the teachers' union would only be counterproductive. Besides, being realistic, an intern would have limited opportunities to solve these problems. You could have focused on the senator's High I personality, but be careful, some people may accuse you of being obsequious. The safest route to us seemed to focus on the applicant's qualities. The hook does hint of your High D personality, doesn't it? You can tell this is a take-charge person. And if the second one hints of High D, the third one screams it.

Example: Hook 6

You desperately want to become a regional manager for a popular fast food chain. You eat their fried chicken all the time and are familiar with their basic operational procedures and management philosophy. Since graduating from college in 1990, you have worked as a restaurant manager for a competing rooster roaster and earned the highly coveted 1991 Cluck-a-Doodle-Doo Manager Award for productivity. You fit under the High I category with some styles of the High C.

Write your hook here:

_____

_____

_____

_____

_____

How about:

- As the 1991 winner of the Cluck-a-Doodle-Doo award at Chickie Littles, I know a little about chicken—and a lot about people.

- Motivating employees to serve the freshest, tastiest chicken quickly and efficiently has made Gizzard's a highly successful chain. Motivating employees to serve the freshest, tastiest chicken quickly and efficiently made me a top restaurant manager with Chickie Littles. I hope to bring my ability to encourage others to your organization as a regional manager.

Try one more practice hook before you write your own. This one is interesting, and, yes, it does work. Remember, it is just as important to think about to whom you are writing as well as what you have to offer the company.

Example: Hook 7

You are a journalism major interested in a career in public relations. Your experiences include a brief stint as a reporter with your school newspaper, an internship with a local newspaper, and a summer job working as a volunteer for a local political candidate. You were also a member of your school's student alumni association and coordinated the annual phone-a-thon to solicit alumni donations. The PR firm you hope to work for is very small but has an excellent reputation in the area and some very powerful clients. You don't know if there is an opening there at this time, but you want to float a resume by them to see if you get a response. You have determined from chapter 3 that the best key words and phrases for you were located under both the High I and High C columns.

Give it a shot:

_____

_____

_____

_____

_____

_____

_____

_____

_____

Writing to a public relations firm seems to us to be a real challenge since you know that your audience consists of people who earn a living writing prose that sells. Consider the following letter:

Dateline: Atlanta, Georgia. December 1, 1993.

PR Company Announces the Addition of Victor Martinez to Its Firm

Victor Martinez is a 1993 graduate of Citytown University, where he majored in communication. As a stringer for the student newspaper, he interviewed

Dr. Abner Borin, professor of theology and the leading theorist on the Lost Ark of the Covenant. That piece was published in *Religion Today* in 1989.

Mr. Martinez's public relations experience includes his tenure as coordinator of the annual alumni fund-raising campaign at Citytown University. As a result of his efforts, a record-breaking $200,000 in donations were made during the campaign. In addition, he contributed to the victory of Mayor Freeman last fall, serving as cochairman of the "Young Voter's for Freeman" initiative.

At PR Company, Mr. Martinez will be working on the Asset Club account, where, as a result of its recent expansion into the competitive field of broadcasting, his organizational skills and creativity will be particularly valuable.

Mr. Martinez is available for interivews and can be reached at (404) 555-5151.

Unusual? Yes, but we are trying to make a point here: a press release submitted to a PR firm instead of the usual cover letter is much more likely to be read and remembered. Even if there is no position available, this candidate will more than likely be interviewed. And if a position becomes available in the future, this person will be the first one called.

That last example is the complete letter: hook, line, and sinker. You begin to see how these elements work together to form a single concept. The hook gets readers' attention. They read the line, and then the information that follows. Before you know it, your audience has reached the end of the letter and the sinker conclusion, which is basically "Call me for an interview—I'm the one!" The reader should be convinced—and without the usual pain and suffering of reading yet another boring letter of introduction. Done well, your letter will flow like a commercial: unified, cohesive, and, with a little extra effort, entertaining.

For some people, the hook will be easier to write after they have written the body, or the line, of the letter. Techniques for writing a solid, informative line are outlined in the next chapter. But first, here are some exercises for you to complete using your key words, phrases, and experiences.

Now It's Your Turn: Your Personal Hook

First, recall your choice of the key words and phrases from chapter 3. Then, consider the company or organization to which you plan to send a cover letter and resume. What personal trait do you think is most applicable to the job position you are seeking?

For example, you fall under the High C category and are applying to a Big 6 accounting firm (High C is not the only style that would succeed at a Big 6). The firm you want to work for most specializes and is most commonly known for its work in computer systems consulting and tax. Your interest is in tax, and you just learned that the firm is increasing its tax staff in your city. It has gone so far as to put an ad in the Sunday paper for an individual tax specialist. You know what this means—300 to possibly 400 resumes will flood the human resource director's office.

Remember from chapter 3 that someone with High C characteristics is analytical and detail oriented and has a high need for perfection. Connect the two, and you get the hook:

> To maintain your standing as the world leader in tax consulting, it is necessary to hire individuals who carefully analyze situations, pay close attention to detail, and are compelled to do things right. I believe I fit this criteria and would succeed as an individual tax specialist with a Big Six accounting firm.

Don't you think this opening gets more attention, says more about yourself, and accomplishes more than simply saying, "I am responding to the ad in the paper?"

Now you try. The following worksheets will help you put together four opening lines. You probably want to use the company names that you worked on in chapter 4.

Exercises: Preparing Your Opening Lines

1 Company name _____

Facts about the company _____

_____

_____

_____

_____

Your personal style most closely related to position for which you are applying _____

_____

_____

_____

_____

_____

Connect the two for your opening to this company _____

_____

_____

_____

_____

_____

_____

2   Company name _____

Facts about the company _____

_____

_____

_____

Your personal style most closely related to position for which you are applying _____

_____

_____

_____

_____

_____

Connect the two for your opening to this company _____

_____

_____

_____

_____

_____

_____

3   Company name _____

Facts about the company _____

_____

_____

_____

Your personal style most closely related to position for which you are applying _____

_____

_____

_____

_____

_____

Connect the two for your opening to this company _____

_____

_____

_____

_____

_____

_____

4   Company name _____

Facts about the company _____

_____

_____

_____

Your personal style most closely related to position for which you are applying _____

_____

_____

_____

_____

_____

Connect the two for your opening to this company _____

_____

_____

_____

_____

_____

_____

Now that you have the attention of the reader, you are ready to move on to the body, or line, of your cover letter. In the next section, you will learn how to tell the reader about your qualifications as well as more about your personal style without losing the reader's attention. Similar exercises will follow, and then you will be ready for the last section: the sinker.

7

The Line

This chapter deals with the information you plan to present to a prospective employer. Call it your sales pitch or your persuasion section, if you prefer. Whatever you call it, the line is the "meat" of your letter.

In part 2 of this book, you explored your personal style, listed your accomplishments, and examined how your style has earned you those accomplishments. You also researched your target employer and discovered facts about what it wants and needs to find in your letter. Armed with these tools and the ability to write a good hook, you are ready to implement the suggestions in this part.

The line of a good cover letter writes itself once you have written a good hook. If you did the exercises in the previous chapter, you are halfway there. If you didn't do them, make it easier on yourself and try them before continuing with this chapter.

Like a well-written commercial, the line is the soft sell. It communicates your selling points without beating the reader over the head about how excellent you are. It is a fine line in some ways—you want to tell them you are great without making them wonder if you are an egomaniac. To accomplish this, you concentrate on the words you choose, their cadence, and their flow. Remember the fast food commercial for a hamburger that listed all of the ingredients from meat to special sauce and ended with the details of the bun? That was the line. The restaurant chain didn't have to say, "Buy our burgers. They're good!" We knew that when everyone in America could recite the entire list just as fast as the actors in the commercials. That is what we want your letter to do—tell them what you need to tell them without sounding like you are telling them.

Okay, you are absolutely right: it is easier to do that in a television commercial, where the wilder you are, the more memorable and successful you are, than in a business letter. But, with practice, you can learn to package yourself in a more dynamic manner.

Example: Line 1

What are you going to tell these people? Why should you work for them? What do you have to offer? Are you 100 percent pure beef, or are you tofu (nothing against tofu—sometimes it's just right)? Do you have experience? Do you have some special skills? Honors? Talent? Good looks? And what can you say that you know the prospective employer wants to hear?

You have to know the required skills, experiences, and abilities as well as your personal profile and employer's view of your presentation before you begin to write the line of your letter. Your resume and what you completed in part 2 of this book should get you started on the first four lines. These are your notes— the seedlings from which mighty persuasion grows. Here is our first example.

You are applying for the research assistant position with the research and development branch of a pharmaceutical company. You have jotted down the following notes:

B.S. in chemistry (honors in my major)

Familiarity with laboratory procedures

Familiar with most popular pharmaceutical-related computer program and word processing software

High C profile—good attention to detail, like the time I was the only one who noticed that Professor Banes misspelled ''hydrochloric acid'' on the final

High C profile—work to perfection, like the senior experiment and report I did on the chemical breakdown of cheeseburgers and got an ''A''

Company research—interested in company's work on AIDS cure I saw in the newspaper

Company research—I use hypoallergenic moisturizer developed by cosmetics division (have tried to recreate it in the lab but couldn't get the percentage of glycerin right)

Additional—had a summer internship with Professor David Shraille as lab assistant; helped him draft a paper entitled ''Five Cents: An Exploration of the Explosive Properties of Nickel.'' Responsibilities included assisting in experiments, answering phones, researching history of nickel experiments. Paper was published in the *Harvard Journal of Pocket Change*. (will use some of these in letter because I heard from a friend that the personnel director has a fit when recent grads think they are too good to do repetitive tasks like answering the phone)

Not all of these notes could or should make it into your letter. But they do give a clear picture of the things you thought of as you sat down to plan your letter. Do these notes look similar to the exercises you completed in chapters 3 and 4?

Once you have made some notes of your own (if you completed the exercises in chapter 3, you already have), read through them and think about the three things that you believe will make the best argument for your cause. And just like in an argument, you have to do more than state the facts to win. A cover letter that repeats your resume is like answering a question with "Becuase I said so!"

In creative writing circles, a popular maxim is "show, don't tell." That commandment is equally applicable here. As you look at this list, think about which of the notes listed show that you have the right stuff: education, experience, enthusiasm, and compatibility for the job. At the end of this chapter, you will complete exercises that will get you started on your first four lines. Do you realize that when you are through with this book, you will have four letters ready to put on bond paper and send in the mail? For now, let's get back to the pharmaceutical example.

You have a degree in a relevant discipline—but that is on your resume. Your familiarity with lab procedures and the applicable technology would be boring if they were just statements made in the body of the letter. But we can show them if we discuss your internship with Dr. Shraille. You assisted him with an experiment that has been published in a well-respected scientific journal, illustrating that you have experience doing the kind of things research assistants do, and these responsibilities might be worth elaborating on in the letter. Your knowledge of a recent accomplishment of the company could show that you have done your homework and that you are thorough, well-informed, and sincere. While this example of your attention to detail is interesting, it might be too cumbersome to relate in this letter. On the other hand, the anecdote about your efforts to duplicate the formula for moisturizer may illustrate this point as well as your devotion to science and be an excellent way to inject a little humor. That might even make a good hook, but we'll consider it as part of the line for the purpose of this exercise. Don't be afraid to choose something a little unusual in your letter—just be sure you handle it with a tactful and light touch. As you are probably aware, not everyone finds the same things funny. As a general rule in your writing, if you are uncomfortable with it, don't use it. For this example, though, let's try to work it in. Although the moisturizer may be an interesting thing to include, the research position is not closely related to cheeseburger disintegration, so maybe you should leave your paper topic in your resume.

So, of the notes listed, your best argument may use the following points: your internship, the company's AIDS research, and your homemade moisturizer.

When you prepare your own list, it will undoubtedly look different. Not everyone has experience as closely related to the job sought as that presented in the example. When that is the case, the list we suggested above is even more important. By listing everything you can think of that has anything at all to do with your qualifications—beyond the information on your resume (your personal profile, for example)—you may discover that you have more to say than you originally imagined. Whether you have long lists of ideas or a short one, pick the three strongest for the line of your letter.

Where's the Beef?

Once you know what you're going to say, the next step is figuring out the best way to say it. Unlike the hook, this section, while still creative, must be more informative. As we said earlier, it is going to be the way you say things that makes a clear and persuasive line.

If you have made a good list, checked it twice, found out what was boring and what was nice, you are ready to continue.

Let's go back to your list.

Knowledge of your target's recent accomplishment
Your experience as a research assistant to a professor
Your moisturizer efforts

Your hook went like this:

Attention to detail, experience, and innovation are the qualities of any good scientist. Add patience and solid computer and laboratory skills and you have an excellent research assistant. I have these skills and hope to put them to work at Chemtech Company.

Now it is your turn. Take our list, and write the line.

_____

_____

_____

_____

_____

_____

_____

_____

_____

_____

_____

_____

_____

This is what we came up with:

Last summer, I assisted Dr. David Shraille with the experiments that resulted in his paper "Five Cents: An Exploration of the Chemical Properties of Nickel," published in the *Harvard Journal of Pocket Change*. As his research assistant, I conducted experiments, maintained the laboratory, performed detailed research assignments, and prepared oral and written reports on various facts related to Dr. Shraille's theses. I developed a working knowledge of the D-base computer system while working for Dr. Shraille.

All aspects of science intrigue me, from cosmetics to the AIDS inoculation research I have read that Chemtech has initiated. In addition to my professional responsibilities, I have conducted several experiments of my own, including an effort to create a moisturizer formula that works as well as the one developed by Chemtech in 1970.

This example flows from the hook and sets you and the reader up for the sinker. It tells the employer the necessary information about your work experience. It says you have all the qualities of the ideal candidate for the job. It states facts about the company Chemtech. And it goes further to say something the personnel director wanted to hear—that you are not too good to maintain the laboratory (this means you cleaned up after the mess made each day). If you remember, you don't want to ignore tasks you didn't like—this personnel director is a stickler for college grads who think they are ready for a position as president. Get the reader to relate. Get him or her to stay interested. Get him or her to call you for an interview.

Easy to say, hard to do, you think? You are right—so practice. Here is another one.

Example: Line 2

You are applying to the State Board of Consumer Affairs to be an investigator. You make a list that includes the following items:

Dad subscribes to *Consumer Reports* and you read it.

You love those consumer television shows where they test out advertising claims and always wanted to try it yourself.

You were once misled by false advertising on TV for an exercise contraption that turned out to be a piece of wire and two rubber bands and broke the first time you used it.

Read a lot of detective stories and watch "Matlock" on TV

Degree in English

Did chapters 3 and 4, determined that the best words and phrases came from the High S and High C lists

That is all you can think of. Your summer job last year was helping out at your Uncle Bill's dairy farm, and while you learned a lot about how to run a farm (and how to rake cow manure), you can't see a way to relate this experience to the job search. Other than watching television, reading, and daydreaming, you have no special experience. Still, the job really appeals to you, and you know that if given the chance, you could really be a first-rate investigator.

With a list like this, we recommend you return to part 2 and review the section on audience. You can probably find out a lot of interesting things about the Office of Consumer Affairs just by calling their receptionist or visiting a branch office. For example, knowing how a complaint is filed or the basic investigative procedure would be impressive facts to add to a letter.

But for the sake of this exercise, let's assume that it is a state holiday, and the office is closed today. You have to submit your application by tomorrow in order to be considered for the job at all, so you have to write your letter with just the notes we set forth. So with that information, you write a hook:

_____

_____

_____

_____

_____

And once you are satisfied with your opening, you review our brief and very unusual list and turn your thoughts toward writing the line for this letter. Remember, a good line flows from the hook and illustrates this applicant's strengths as well as points out what the reader wants to see. Go to it!

_____

_____

_____

_____

_____

_____

_____

_____

_____

_____

_____

_____

Which facts does your line talk about? It really doesn't matter what you chose if you were able to roll it together into a cohesive and persuasive argument for your employment. This is what we came up with:

> In our consumer society, the average individual is bombarded with advertisements for all kinds of products, many of which do not live up to their claims. My interest in public service and consumer issues and my analytical skills will enable me to investigate incidents of consumer fraud thoroughly and well.

> As an English major, I developed strong language and writing skills that a good investigator needs to succeed. Fact finding, collecting evidence, interviewing individuals, and analyzing information are abilities I can bring to this position. I am well read on consumer issues and have a working knowledge of a range of consumer offenses from mail fraud to odometer fraud.

This example puts the limited information in our list to the best possible use. It uses facts about the consumer society and personal profile traits (in this person's case, High C style), it mentions qualifications (the English major), and it says something the prospective employer wants to hear (fact-finding, collecting evidence). The problem with this example is that no matter how cleverly it is written, it is still vague. One concrete example could change it substantially. For example, if you visited the consumer affairs office and learned about how complaints were filed, you could say:

When a consumer files a complaint, he or she may not provide enough details about the incident or list all of the parties that he or she believes were involved. It is the investigator's responsibility to ''fill in the blanks.'' My fact-finding, interviewing, and analytical abilities as well as my degree in English mean that I can flesh out the details of the charge and draft it into a coherent final investigative report.

Can you see the difference it makes to have some knowledge about the job, its lingo, and standard operating procedures? The more you know, the longer your list, and the better your line.

Example: Line 3

Let's return to the example about the senior at State Tech who majored in computer science and finance whose father wants him to become a banker. The following is a list of facts that you would have written.

Senior at State Tech, will graduate in spring of 1993

Majored in computer science and finance

Worked on D-base program under the direction of the head of computer science department at Tech

Senior programming project focused on innovative D-base programming for international financial service-based industry

Dad is a banker

Read in Dad's *Citywide Banker's Journal* that local bank is currently implementing Zinc Software, Inc.'s new D-base program

Used D-base language for recent class project

Dad wants me to become a banker

I want to work with computers

Best phrases were under High D and High C

Our hook went like this:

Implementing Zinc Software Company's new D-base program requires not only patience and attention to detail by those responsible for downloading the entire system but leadership skills as well. I believe I fit this criteria and could help Metro Bank efficiently implement Zinc's innovative D-base program as well as maintain your corporate information system.

Write the line for this letter using your list of important facts and taking advantage of personal style.

_____

_____

_____

_____

_____

_____

_____

_____

_____

_____

_____

Here is ours. Remember, our line is not the best nor is it the only way to convey the important facts. You know what is important for you and your readers. Yours could be longer, shorter, or broken into bullet points. We thought this was short and to the point.

For my senior programming project, I developed an internationl financial service database program written in the same language as Zinc's new program. By understanding its language and committing myself to hard work, I could help tailor this new program to fit the particular needs of Metro Bank and troubleshoot any problems that arise in the future.

In the next example, we refer to our advanced-degree candidate. In this example, you have a master's degree in social psychology and communication and want to make Emerging Communication Technologies, Inc., a leader in the international market for communications.

Example: Line 4

The following is a list of facts that you though were worthwhile enough to discuss in the cover letter.

Graduate of Citytown University School of Mass Communication

Master's degree in social psychology and communication

Worked for over one year as a management consultant at AceCorp Consulting

Liaison and assistant to managing partner of firm

Worked on international accounts like BellWorld, ZZ&B, DPB Cellular

Master's thesis: "International Business Failures: Are They Our Products or Our Presentation?"

Love to make speeches and talk with people

High I words and phrases

Emerging Communication Technologies, Inc., has been rated as one of *Fortune* magazine's up-and-comer Fortune 500 companies with the introduction of its new satellite

Seems like an excellent opportunity to get in on the ground floor

Our hook went like this:

A concise and accurate presentation is only the first step toward convincing international officials to invest in Emerging Communication Technologies, Inc.'s new satellite. Persuasive arguments that show ECT will benefit those countries without disrupting their cultures will, undoubtedly, position your company as a leader in the field. With a master's degree in social psychology and communication as well as experience in the communications field, I can help successfully market your new satellite.

Write the line for this letter. Remember, you are trying to convince the reader that you have excellent communication skills and that you know something about the international market.

_____

_____

_____

_____

_____

_____

_____

_____

_____

_____

_____

_____

Ours went like this:

> As the assistant to the managing partner at AceCorp Consulting, I have had the opportunity to develop my communication skills in several areas. During firm partner meetings, for example, I present potential client marketing strategies that I helped develop. At the client level, I facilitate the implementation of all marketing plans designed by our firm by preparing correspondence and answering any questions the client may have. Working as the firm's liaison, I maintain a computerized client database, write confirm letters, and prepare service information packages.
>
> While earning a master's degree in Social Psychology and mass communication at Citytown University, I focused my thesis on international business failures. In my thesis, I address the problems of presentation and communication and have successfully applied my theories while working with AceCorp clients like BellWorld, ZZ&B, and DPB Cellular.

Notice that the line of this letter started out discussing your present job and qualifications and ended by saying something particularly relevant to the reader. This should keep the reader until the very end and will convey that the applicant knows what he or she is talking about. The key is to keep the reader interested. Tell them enough to keep them wanting more, which you will be happy to share—during an interview perhaps.

Example: Line 5

Some more facts about the job with Senator Richard D. Cobb:

Majored in political science

High D words and phrases

Senator is High I

Embattled with National Teachers' Union over policy

President of SGA senior year

Student-alumni embassador

Ambitious

Driven

Overachiever

Obnoxious (sometimes)

Our hook went like this:

Initiative. A simple word. With it, nothing is impossible. Without it, all is lost.

Write the line for this letter. What do you think is important?

_____

_____

_____

_____

_____

_____

_____

_____

_____

_____

_____

_____

Our line:

Fact: Led the annual alumni fund-raising drive, 1991–92, achieving a total in $230,543 in donations.

Fact: Served as president of the Student Government Association, 1991–92. Appointed student committee to implement AIDS awareness program on campus. Supported initiative to recruit student volunteers to participate in activities with local high schools to provide motivation and teacher support.

Fact: Political science major, with concentrations in American government and political processes.

Fact: Leader. Driven. Results oriented.

This line is more unusual than the others we have discussed so far. But it suits both the audience and the position. Let's face it: internships of this sort are highly competitive, so you really have to work hard to create a lasting impression. Furthermore, someone interested in public life needs to demonstrate an ability to be innovative and dynamic when faced with obstacles. This line conveys those strengths.

Example: Line 6

For our last exercise, let's write the line for the applicant who hopes to transfer from Chickie Littles to Gizzards. Here are some facts to go on:

Experienced restaurant manager

Motivator

People person

Cluck-a-Doodle-Doo award, 1991

Here is the hook we provide for this letter:

As the 1991 winner of the Cluck-a-Doodle-Doo award at Chickie Littles, I know a little about chicken—and a lot about people.

Write the line for this letter. What qualities should a regional manager focus on in the cover letter?

_____

_____

_____

_____

_____

_____

_____

_____

_____

_____

_____

_____

Our line:

The best regional managers know what really goes on in a fast food restaurant: employees who are often late or fail to show at all, the pitfalls of the lunch and dinner peak hours, the lessons of supply and demand.

I earned the Cluck-a-Doodle-Doo award after two years of managing a busy store in the heart of Citytown. I can sympathize with the struggles of the restaurant manager and motivate him or her to greater success and higher profits.

Notice that this letter demonstrates the best of the qualities of the High I style: outgoing, concerned with people and their problems, and a solid presentational ability. It outlines this candidate's experiences and illustrates his or her ability to motivate and persuade.

The next exercises give you the opportunity to put together four lines which follow the four hooks you prepared in the last chapter.

Your Turn: Prepare the Line for Your Letter

Complete the following four worksheets, and you will be ready to begin working on the finale, the sinker of your letters.

Worksheet 1

Copy the first hook you prepared in the last chapter. _____

_____

_____

_____

_____

_____

What are the three most important points you need to discuss in the line for this
letter? Include (1) experiences and qualifications and how your personal style has
earned these; (2) something that you believe the reader wants or needs to hear in
order to stay interested—remember the stickler for recent grads example; and
(3) facts about the company that you could relate to the first and second points.
Look at the exercises you completed in chapters 3 and 4.

Point 1 _____

_____

_____

_____

_____

Point 2 _____

_____

_____

_____

_____

Point 3 _____

_____

_____

_____

_____

Construct the line that would incorporate these three points. Make sure it
follows coherently from your hook.

_____

_____

_____

_____

_____

_____

_____

_____

_____

_____

_____

_____

_____

Worksheet 2

Copy the second hook you prepared in the last chapter. _____

_____

_____

_____

_____

_____

What are the three most important points you need to discuss in the line for this letter? Include (1) experiences and qualifications and how your personal style has earned these; (2) something that you believe the reader wants or needs to hear in order to stay interested—remember the stickler for recent grads example; and (3) facts about the company that you could relate to the first and second points. Look at the exercises you completed in chapters 3 and 4.

Point 1 _____

_____

_____

_____

Point 2 _____

_____

_____

_____

Point 3 _____

_____

_____

_____

_____

Construct the line that would incorporate these three points. Make sure it
follows coherently from your hook.

_____

_____

_____

_____

_____

_____

_____

_____

_____

_____

_____

_____

_____

Worksheet 3

Copy the third hook you prepared in the last chapter. _____

_____

_____

_____

_____

_____

What are the three most important points you need to discuss in the line for this letter? Include (1) experiences and qualifications and how your personal style has earned these; (2) something that you believe the reader wants or needs to hear in order to stay interested—remember the stickler for recent grads example; and (3) facts about the company that you could relate to the first and second points. Look at the exercises you completed in chapters 3 and 4.

Point 1 _____

_____

_____

_____

_____

Point 2 _____

_____

_____

_____

_____

Point 3 _____

_____

Construct the line that would incorporate these three points. Make sure it
follows coherently from your hook.

Worksheet 4

Copy the fourth hook you prepared in the last chapter. _____

_____

_____

_____

_____

What are the three most important points you need to discuss in the line for this letter? Include (1) experiences and qualifications and how your personal style has earned these; (2) something that you believe the reader wants or needs to hear in order to stay interested—remember the stickler for recent grads example; and (3) facts about the company that you could relate to the first and second points. Look at the exercises you completed in chapters 3 and 4.

Point 1 _____

_____

_____

_____

Point 2 _____

_____

_____

_____

Point 3 _____

_____

_____

_____

_____

Construct the line that would incorporate these three points. Make sure it
follows coherently from your hook.

_____

_____

_____

_____

_____

_____

_____

_____

_____

_____

_____

_____

_____

We have discussed the hook and the line. You should be beginning to see how these elements combine to inject your letter with the kind of enthusiasm and energy that distinguishes you from the crowd. Think about it—you almost have four complete cover letters. Now it is time to move to the finale, which we call the sinker.

8

The Sinker

You caught them with the hook. You fed them with the line. Now it is time to polish them off with the sinker. This is your closing paragraph and your recap.

Let's go back to our analogy of a commercial. You have noticed that commercials always end with a repetition of the product and the slogan or jingle that is being used to sell the product. It is a recap of what the advertiser wants you to remember. You want a prospective employer to remember something about you before he or she goes on to the next letter in the pile, but like a commercial, this should be a repetition of something you have said about yourself earlier. In other words, you are recapping your selling points. So before the sinker, you should go back and re-read your hook and line. As you read, look for a theme, word, quality, or experience. It may jump out at you. Like the slogan of a commercial. Try to keep the repetition as short as possible, like in a commercial message. It is not memorable if you repeat half your line—it is just lazy. The sinker is no more than a sentence of probably only a few words.

There are some things that you should work into your closing paragraphs, regardless of its sinker elements. As briefly as possible, tell your prospective employer how to reach you; when you will call to follow up; and thank him or her.

But this is also a good opportunity to make one final pitch about one of the points you made earlier in either your hook or your line. Sometimes, instead of lumping each of these items into one long paragraph, you might want to separate them into two or even three paragraphs. We will discuss that possibility when we do some examples.

Let's write some sinkers for the lines from the previous section. Remember our

89

examples about working for a pharmaceutical company? Your hook and line went like this:

Example: Sinker 1

Attention to detail, experience, and innovation are the qualities of any good scientist. Add patience and solid computer and laboratory skills, and you have an excellent research assistant. I have these skills and hope to put them to work at Chemtech Company.

Last summer, I assisted Dr. David Shraille with the experiments that resulted in his paper ''Five Cents: An Exploration of the Chemical Properties of Nickel,'' published in the *Harvard Journal of Pocket Change*. As his research assistant, I conducted experiments, maintained the laboratory, performed detailed research assignments, and prepared oral and written reports on various facts related to Dr. Shraille's theses. I developed a working knowledge of the D-base computer system while working for Dr. Shraille.

All aspects of science intrigue me, from cosmetics to the AIDS inoculation research I have read that Chemtech has initiated. In addition to my professional responsibilities, I have conducted several experiments of my own, including an effort to create a moisturizer formula that works as well as the one developed by Chemtech in 1970.

As you read your hook and line, list the words and phrases that best sum up your qualifications and abilities here:

_____

_____

_____

_____

_____

Our list looks like this:

- Attention to detail, experience, and innovation
- Good scientist
- Patience, computer and lab skills

- Science intrigues you

- Initiates own experiments

- Wide interest in various disciplines

Your list might be longer or shorter depending on what you find significant about the hook and the line.

Once again, our task is to determine which phrases will most help you achieve your goal: the position of research assistant at Chemtech. What will Chemtech want most in a research assistant? A moisturizer maker? Someone with wide interests? Or will it be a good scientist with experience and computer and lab skills? What matters most here—your personal style or your work history?

Probably you could write a good sinker with either approach. If you wanted to concentrate on your personal style, you might write a sinker like this:

Attention to detail, experience, patience, and initiative—these are the qualities of a good scientist and research assistant. They are qualities I possess and hope to demonstrate in my employment with Chemtech. You may reach me at (404) 555-1143.

Thank you for considering me.

On the other hand, you could choose to concentrate on experience by writing a sinker like this:

My experiences with Dr. Shraille and my familiarity with laboratory procedures, software, and the research that accompanies experimentation in developing fields of science will enable me to assume a full work load at Chemtech immediately. For a personal reference, you may contact Dr. Shraille at (404) 555-9856; I can be reached at (404) 555-1143.

Thank you for considering me.

Both of these sinkers are perfectly fine. They recap the salient points of the writer's hook and line nicely, repeating that he or she is experienced and well qualified to assume the position sought. Notice that we didn't choose to talk about the moisturizer incident. While your letter should be memorable, it has to be memorable for the right reasons. Employers should remember how confident and intelligent you are, not how offbeat you are. For this job, humor and creativity should be secondary goals. In other circumstances (like applying for a position in public relations, advertising, art) the more unusual the sinker, the better your chances. As we discussed earlier, it all depends on your intended audience.

Don't get the sinker confused with the hook. Their purposes are completely different. The hook, by its very definition, has to be eye-catching and attention getting. If it is not, chances are the reader will throw the letter aside, scan the resume, and move on to the next one in the pile. A good hook prevents that from happening. You don't need to be as dramatic with the sinker. You already have the attention of your audience, but you want to make absolutely certain that the reader remembers your best points. In other words, the sinker hits your audience over the head with your amazing talents and qualifications one more time. It is a short summary, but well written and interesting like the rest of your letter.

Example: Sinker 2

Let's write the sinker for another of our earlier exercises. Remember in the last chapter, you wrote the hook and line for a cover letter applying to the State Office of Consumer Affairs. We provide this version:

> In our consumer society, the average individual is bombarded with advertisements for all kinds of products, many of which do not live up to their claims. My interest in public service and consumer issues and my analytical skills will enable me to investigate incidents of consumer fraud thoroughly and well.
>
> As an English major, I developed strong language and writing skills which are necessary for a good investigator. Fact-finding, collecting evidence, interviewing individuals, and analyzing information are abilities I can bring to this position. I am well read on consumer issues and have a working knowledge of a range of consumer offenses from mail fraud to odometer fraud.

Make a list of the key words and phrases from the hook and line:

_____

_____

_____

_____

_____

Now finish up with a sinker:

_____

_____

_____

_____

Here is what we did:

- Public service, interest in consumer affairs
- Analytical and writing skills
- Fact-finding, collecting evidence, interviewing
- Well read, knowledge on consumer offenses

Our sinker:

I hope you will contact me at (404) 555-6576 if you need any additional information about me or how my analytical and investigative skills fit with your objectives. Thank you.

or:

My knowledge of and enthusiasm about consumer issues, combined with my desire to begin a career in public service, make me an excellent candidate for investigator with your office. Please do not hesitate to contact me at (404) 555-6576 if you need any additional information from me. I hope to hear from you soon. Thank you.

Notice that in this one, we lumped all of our closing information into one paragraph. Why? It seemed to flow well that way. Use your judgment about when to separate phone numbers and thank you's from the rest of your letter. Generally, if you sinker is short, you can combine it with additional closing information relatively easily. A longer sinker, however, should be separated from the other elements of your letter's finale. Additional closing phrases are discussed in more detail in following examples.

By now, you are probably beginning to understand how the sinker works to tie in the best your hook and line have to offer.

Example: Sinker 3

Now let's write the sinker for the computer specialist applying to a bank. Our hook and line went like this:

Implementing Zinc Software Company's new D-base program requires not only patience and attention to detail by those responsible for downloading the entire system but leadership skills as well. I believe I fit this criteria and could help Metro Bank efficiently implement Zinc's innovative D-base program as well as maintain your corporate information system.

For my senior programming project, I developed an international financial service database program written in the same language as Zinc's new program. By understanding its language and committing myself to hard work, I could help tailor this new program to fit the particular needs of Metro Bank and troubleshoot any problems that arise in the future.

Make a list of the key words and phrases from this hook and line:

_____

_____

_____

_____

_____

Now finish up with a sinker:

_____

_____

_____

_____

_____

_____

_____

_____

Here is our list:

- International financial services program

- Worked on program in same language as Zinc Software

- Attentive to detail; leader

Our sinker:

I look forward to putting my expertise to work at Metro Bank and hope to meet you soon. You can reach me at (703) 555-2010. Thank you.

This isn't as outlandish as some of the other examples. But remember, this person is applying for a position in banking and computers. You don't close a letter to a bank with "hasta la vista, baby!!"

Example: Sinker 4

Now consider our advanced-degree candidate's hook and line.

A concise and accurate presentation is only the first step toward convincing international officials to invest in Emerging Communication Technologies, Inc.'s new satellite. Persuasive arguments that show ECT will benefit those countries without disrupting their cultures will, undoubtedly, position your company as a leader in the field. With a master's degree in social psychology and communication as well as experience in the communications field, I can help successfully market your new satellite.

As the assistant to the managing partner at AceCorp Consulting, I have had the opportunity to develop my communication skills in several areas. During firm partner meetings, for example, I present potential client marketing strategies that I helped develop. At the client level, I facilitate the implementation of all marketing plans designed by our firm by preparing correspondence and answering any questions the client may have. Working as the firm's liaison, I maintain a computerized client database, write confirmation letters, and prepare service information packages.

While earning a master's degree in social psychology and mass communication at Citytown University, I focused my thesis on international business failures. In my thesis, I address the problems of presentation and communication and have successfully applied my theories while working with AceCorp clients like BellWorld, ZZ&B, and DPB Cellular.

Make a list of the key words and phrases from the hook and line:

_____

_____

_____

_____

_____

Now finish up with a sinker:

_____

_____

_____

_____

_____

_____

_____

_____

Our list looks like this:

- Full-time experience in management consulting
- Educational emphasis on international marketing
- Ability to interact well with different people

Here is our sinker:

With my background in management consulting, my educational emphasis on the international business sector, and my ability to interact well with different people, I believe I can help ECT reach its goals. You can reach me at (404) 555-9876.

Thank you.

Notice that we included both experience and personal style in this closing. We separated the "thank you" simply because it worked better.

Example: Sinker 5

Write the sinker to Senator Richard D. Cobb. Here is the hook and line we provided:

Initiative. A simple word. With it, nothing is impossible. Without it, all is lost.

Fact: Led the annual alumni fund-raising drive, 1991–92, achieving a total in $230,543 in donations.

Fact: Served as president of the Student Government Association, 1991–92. Appointed student committee to implement AIDS awareness on campus. Supported initiative to recruit student volunteers to participate in activities with local high schools to provide motivation and teacher support.

Fact: Political science major, with concentrations in American government and political processes.

Fact: Leader. Driven. Results oriented.

Make a list of the key words and phrases from the hook and line:

_____

_____

_____

_____

_____

This is what we came up with:

- Initiative

- Fund raiser

- President of Student Government Association

- Political science major

- Leader

- Driven
- Results oriented

Now finish up with the sinker:

_____

_____

_____

_____

_____

_____

_____

_____

How about this:

Initiative.

"What?" you're screaming. You can't do that! Where is the phone number? Where is the polite "thank you?" This cover letter is breaking all the rules.

You are right. It does break all the rules. But it works.

It is dramatic. It is interesting. It gets the reader's attention and holds it. It conveys all kinds of useful information about the applicant. And if you remember what we talked about in chapter 4, you have your address and phone number prominently placed on the top of your cover letter and resume. And somehow, "thank you" doesn't close this letter nearly as effectively.

A word of warning: you can't break the rules until you have mastered them. For those of you who are beginning to get the hang of it, this letter is another example of how creative you can be and still be within the limits of acceptable business correspondence.

Now let's do one last sinker. We'll be a little more conservative this time.

Example: Sinker 6

Finish up by preparing the closing for the restaurant regional manager. Here is the hook and line we provided:

As the 1991 winner of the Cluck-a-Doodle-Doo award at Chickie Littles, I know a little about chicken—and a lot about people.

The best regional managers know what really goes on in a fast food restaurant: employees who are often late or fail to show at all, the pitfalls of the lunch and dinner peak hours, the lessons of supply and demand.

I earned the Cluck-a-Doodle-Doo award after two years of managing a busy store in the heart of Citytown. I can sympathize with the struggles of the restaurant manager and motivate him or her to greater success and higher profits.

Make a list of the key words and phrases from the hook and line:

_____

_____

_____

_____

Here is our list
- Experience
- Knowledge
- Chicken
- People

Now finish up with a sinker:

_____

_____

_____

_____

_____

_____

And finally, ours:

Although my experience is with a competitor, my demonstrated knowledge of the industry makes me an excellent candidate. Won't you consider me?

You can reach me at (316) 555-9268.

Thank you.

We tried a slightly different approach here with the question "Won't you consider me?" Although you don't want to sound desperate (even when you are), this letter doesn't convey that impression. Instead, the writer sounds like a friendly, optimistic, and enthusiastic person—exactly the qualities that this employer will be looking for in a regional manager. Additionally, any hint of silliness or flippancy this closing might arouse is counterbalanced by this candidate's qualifications.

By now, you should be starting to see how important it is to know who your audience is and what the position you seek entails. Only then can you know when to be conservative and when to be bold.

Closing Thoughts

Finally, here are a few words about closings in general. Even if your phone number appears on your resume and under your address at the top of the letter, it is a good idea to repeat it in the closing. You never know—after reading your fantastic, creative letter, the employer may just want to call to set up your interview right away. Make it easier for them—tell them again! Of course, that is just a rule of thumb and, as we are fond of saying, rules were made to be broken.

You should always thank your reader at some point in the last few sentences of the letter. "Thank you for considering me" or just simply "Thank you" is enough. Don't get overly profuse. "Thank you for your time and consideration" sounds like you don't think what you had to say was worth the time spent reading it. "Thank you for reading this letter" sounds like you didn't expect your reader to finish. Give yourself some credit.

A sentence about your intentions to follow up is good but not strictly necessary. With or without it, you can make a follow-up telephone call about a week after you have submitted your letter, just to remind the prospective employer of your existence and get some information about how and when interviews will be scheduled and how long it will take for a decision to be reached. Keep your call brief. And don't say in your letter that you will call on a specific day or time. The person who read your letter probably won't be there. Say "next week" or "in a few days."

It's Your Turn Again: Prepare Your Sinker

Using the hooks and lines you prepared in the last chapter, construct the finale for each. Prepare the sinkers:

Sinker 1 _____

_____

_____

_____

_____

Sinker 2 _____

_____

_____

_____

_____

Sinker 3 _____

_____

_____

_____

_____

_____

Sinker 4 _____

_____

_____

_____

_____

Summary

And there you have it: hook, line, and sinker. These are the basic tools for writing an unforgettable cover letter that will distinguish you from the hundreds of other applicants submitting similar resumes.

You are probably thinking that you understand how to do this, and you can see how it will help you write a better letter. But can it really help you get more interviews?

Absolutely!

Appendix A:
Sample Cover
Letters

P.O. Box 480
Citytown University
Citytown, USA 12345
(505) 645-5565

April 10, 1993

Ms. Ann Jones
Recruiting Director
The Acme Company
800 South Main Street
Citytown, USA 12345

Dear Ms. Jones:

As a result of Acme Company's recent acquisition of Foodstuff International, employees with knowledge of restaurant management and food service would be a particular asset to your company. My experiences managing a snack shop, my degree in business administration, and my internship with Apex Company make me an ideal candidate for Acme's management trainee program.

At Citytown University, I served as president of the Young Professional's Club. I was responsible for Eats, a snack bar that catered to college students. Under my direction, Eats initiated a coupon book and a daily specials program which increased the restaurant's profitability by 15 percent.

Through my internship with Apex, I was exposed to other aspects of business, including Apex's new computerized data access system. I believe that the skills I developed during my internship would transfer easily to Acme. Furthermore, these experiences illustrate my ability to quickly master new concepts and assume complex responsibilities.

My resume is included with this letter, but I will contact you next week to answer any questions you may have about me or my background.

I look forward to talking with you about myself, Eats, and how I can become a part ot the Acme Company. Thank you.

Sincerely

Jane Doe

April 10, 1993

Julie B. Graduate
650 Main Street
Citytown, USA 12345
(202) 555-0954

Citytown University
Office of Human Resources
40013 Haverford Building
Citytown, USA 12435

Dear Madam or Sir:

Because Citytown has recently adopted a local area network linking all
campus terminals, a basic familiarity with computers will be an important
criterion for new employees. As my resume indicates, I have experience with
computers as well as a degree in accounting and have applicable work
experience.

Interacting with people has always been one of my strongest attributes. During
my tenure as president of Beta Alpha Psi, a national accounting honor society,
I coordinated the guest speaker lecture series, including two hiring partners
from Citytown's largest accounting firms and the controller from a Fortune
100 company.

As a member of the student activities budget committee, I was responsible for
reconciling the annual budget and dispersing funds to select organizations.
This function, as well as my ability to interact well with others, seems to
match closely with the description you have provided about the administrative
assistant position.

As you can see, I have the necessary skills and the personality to succeed as
an administrative assistant. Please contact me if you would like to further
discuss how I could contribute to Citytown University. You can reach me at
(202) 555-0954.

Thank you.

Sincerely,

Julie B. Graduate

5856 Money Drive
Dollartown, USA 10000
(707) 555-9987

April 10, 1993

Professional Staffing
Moxie, Inc.
1001 Uptown Place
Dollartown, USA 10001

RE: Stockbroker Trainee Program

Dear Madam or Sir:

Ambition, drive, and foresight. These are the qualities that characterize Moxie, Inc., and its employees. As my resume shows, these are qualities I possess and hope to implement as a stockbroker trainee with your company.

The following is a brief summary of my qualifications:

Ambition: As a junior at Ivy League University, I was the first student in the history of the school to be elected president of the Student Government Association and as the representative to the University Board of Trustees.

Drive: While working as an intern for the U.S. Financial Group, I helped meet a crucial deadline on a project for one of the company's largest clients by working into the early morning hours to correct a system failure that had the potential of setting us back two weeks.

Foresight: As an avid stock market follower, I suggested several investments for my parents, who, after following my advice, showed a 16 percent return on their investments last year.

As a stockbroker trainee with your firm, I would continue to maintain these standards as well as the values set forth by Moxie, Inc. To arrange an interview, please call me at (707) 555-9987. I look forward to hearing from you.

Thank you.

Most sincerely,

Will B. Rich

Dateline: Atlanta, Georgia. April 10, 1993.

PR Company Announces the Addition of Victor Martinez to Its Firm

Victor Martinez is a 1991 graduate of Citytown University, where he majored in communication. As a stringer for the student newspaper, he interviewed Dr. Abner Borin, professor of theology and the leading theorist on the Lost Ark of the Covenant. That piece was published in *Religion Today* in 1989.

Mr. Martinez's public relations experience includes his tenure as coordinator of the annual alumni fund-raising campaign at Citytown University. As a result of his efforts, a record-breaking $200,000 in donations were made during the campaign. In addition, he contributed to the victory of Mayor Freeman last fall, serving as cochairman of the "Young Voter's for Freeman" initiative.

At PR Company, Mr. Martinez will be working on the Asset Club account, where, as a result of its recent expansion into the competitive field of broadcasting, his organizational skills and creativity will be particularly valuable.

Victor Martinez is available for interviews and can be reached at (404) 555-5151.

P.O. Box 22071
Accounting Business School
New City, USA 23234
(505) 555-3549

Hiring Partner
Giant & Co., CPA
1400 Glass Tower
240 Prestige Street
New City, USA 24343-1400

Dear Reader:

To maintain your standing as the world leader in tax consulting, it is necessary to hire individuals who carefully analyze situations, pay close attention to detail, and are compelled to do things right. I believe I fit this criteria and would succeed as an individual tax specialist with Giant & Co.

While working in the accounting department of ABC Corporation last summer, I was responsible for reviewing the working papers of each subsidiary. By the end of the summer, I had corrected several important figures that would have otherwise been stated incorrectly in the consolidated financials of the annual report.

As you can see on my resume, I have earned a cumulative grade point average of 3.75 and a 3.93 in my major.

After graduation, I hope to take full advantage of my work experience as well as the many hours I put in studying accounting and finance by starting my career with Giant & Co. Please call me at (505) 555-3549 to discuss arranging an interview. Thank you for your consideration.

Cordially,

Irwin R. Steadman

Renee C. Winford
65 Oaktown Drive
Mytown, USA 32345
(404) 555-1143

April 10, 1993

Dr. R. Thomas
Chemtech Corporation
750 Research Parkway
Suite 987
Research, USA 75847

Dear Dr. Thomas:

Attention to detail, experience, and innovation are the qualities of any good scientist. Add patience and solid computer and laboratory skills, and you have an excellent research assistant. I have these skills and hope to put them to work at Chemtech Company.

Last summer, I assisted Dr. David Shraille with the experiments that resulted in his paper "Five Cents: An Exploration of the Chemical Properties of Nickel," published in the *Harvard Journal of Pocket Change*. As his research assistant, I conducted experiments, maintained the laboratory, performed detailed research assignments, and prepared oral and written reports on various facts related to Dr. Shraille's theses. I developed a working knowledge of the D-base computer system while working for Dr. Shraille.

All aspects of science intrigue me, from cosmetics to the AIDS inoculation research I have read that Chemtech has initiated. In addition to my professional responsibilities, I have conducted several experiments of my own, including an effort to create a moisturizer formula that works as well as the one developed by Chemtech in 1970.

Attention to detail, experience, patience, and initiative—these are the qualities of a good scientist and research assistant. They are qualities I possess and hope to demonstrate in my employment with Chemtech. You may reach me at (404) 555-1143.

Thank you for considering me.

Sincerely,

Renee C. Winford

575 Relax Street
Anywhere, USA 48765
(404) 555-6576
April 10, 1993

Senior Investigating Officer
Investigative Offices International
555 Looking Glass Drive
Political City, USA 12323

Dear Employer:

When a consumer files a complaint, he or she may not provide enough details about the incident or list all of the parties that he or she believes were involved. It is the investigator's responsibility to "fill in the blanks." My fact-finding, interviewing, and analytical abilities as well as my degree in English mean that I can flesh out the details of the charge and draft it into a coherent final investigative report.

As an English major, I developed strong language and writing skills which are necessary for a good investigator. Fact-finding, collecting evidence, interviewing individuals, and analyzing information are abilities I can bring to this position. I am well read on consumer issues and have a working knowledge of a range of consumer offenses from mail fraud to odometer fraud.

My knowledge of and enthusiasm about consumer issues, combined with my desire to begin a career in public service, make me an excellent candidate for investigator with your office. Please do not hesitate to contact me at (404) 555-6576 if you need any additional information from me. I hope to hear from you soon. Thank you.

Respectfully,

Howard R. Seek

124 Tech Drive
City Tech University
Banker Town, USA 44444
(703) 555-2010

April 10, 1993

Recruiting Coordinator
Metro Bank National
Plaza One
Suite 1700
Banker Town, USA 44455

Dear Sir or Madam:

Implementing Zinc Software Company's new D-base program requires not only patience and attention to detail by those responsible for downloading the entire system but leadership skills as well. I believe I fit this criteria and could help Metro Bank efficiently implement Zinc's innovative D-base program as well as maintain your corporate information system.

For my senior programming project, I developed an international financial service database program written in the same language as Zinc's new program. By understanding its language and committing myself to hard work, I could help tailor this new program to fit the particular needs of Metro Bank and troubleshoot any problems that arise in the future.

I look forward to putting my expertise to work at Metro Bank and hope to meet you soon. You can reach me at (703) 555-2010. Thank you.

Sincerely,

Stephen C. Waters

Thelma L. Bouvier
55 Parkside Drive
Citytown, USA 44435
(404) 555-9876

April 10, 1993

Heidi M. Feldman, President
Emerging Market Communications, Inc.
100 Technology Parkway
Suite 700
Technology, USA 00001

Dear Ms. Feldman:

A concise and accurate presentation is only the first step toward convincing international officials to invest in Emerging Communication Technologies, Inc.'s new satellite. Persuasive arguments that show ECT will benefit those countries without disrupting their cultures will, undoubtedly, position your company as a leader in the field. With a master's degree in social psychology and communication as well as experience in the communications field, I can help successfully market your new satellite.

As the assistant to the managing partner at AceCorp Consulting, I have had the opportunity to develop my communication skills in several areas. During firm partner meetings, for example, I present potential client marketing strategies that I helped develop. At the client level, I facilitate the implementation of all marketing plans designed by our firm by preparing correspondence and answering any questions the client may have. Working as the firm's liaison, I maintain a computerized client database, write confirmation letters, and prepare service information packages.

While earning a master's degree in social psychology and mass communication at Citytown University, I focused my thesis on international business failures. In my thesis, I address the problems of presentation and communication and have successfully applied my theories while working with AceCorp clients like BellWorld, ZZ&B, and DPB Cellular.

With my background in management consulting, my educational emphasis on the international business sector, and my ability to interact well with different people, I believe I can help ECT reach its goals. You can reach me at (404) 555-9876.

Thank you.

Sincerely,

Thelma L. Bouvier

Mark T. Butterman
809 Tillim Avenue
Washington, DC 10003
(202) 555-6673

April 10, 1993

Senator Richard D. Cobb
Capitol Building Annex
Suite 101
Washington, DC 10001

Dear Senator Cobb:

Initiative. A simple word. With it, nothing is impossible. Without it, all is lost.

Fact: Led the annual alumni fund-raising drive, 1991–92, achieving a total in $230,543 in donations.

Fact: Served as president of the Student Government Association, 1991–92. Appointed student committee to implement AIDS awareness on campus. Supported initiative to recruit student volunteers to participate in activities with local high schools to provide motivation and teacher support.

Fact: Political science major, with concentrations in American government and political processes.

Fact: Leader. Driven. Results oriented.

Initiative.

Yours truly,

Mark T. Butterman

Steven H. Rothchild
455 Hackensack Drive
Citytown, USA 45443
(316) 555-9268

April 10, 1993

Howard H. Townsend
Area Manager - Southeast
Gizzard's Chicken House, Inc.
455 Gizzard Plaza
Citytown, USA 45432

Dear Mr. Townsend:

As the 1991 winner of the Cluck-a-Doodle-Doo award at Chickie Littles, I know a little about chicken—and a lot about people.

The best regional managers know what really goes on in a fast food restaurant: employees who are often late or fail to show at all, the pitfalls of the lunch and dinner peak hours, the lessons of supply and demand.

I earned the Cluck-a-Doodle-Doo award after two years of managing a busy store in the heart of Citytown. I can sympathize with the struggles of the restaurant manager and motivate him or her to greater success and higher profits.

Although my experience is with a competitor, my demonstrated knowledge of the industry makes me an excellent candidate. Won't you consider me?

You can reach me at (316) 555-9268.

Thank you.

Sincerely,

Steven H. Rothchild

Appendix B: Additional Resources

Below is a list of source books you might find helpful both in the job search generally and in writing your cover letter. Most books should be available in your local or college library, and we have included the Library of Congress call numbers where available to make it easier for you to find them there. Others can be found in most bookstores.

The list is divided into topics—everything from resume help to basic grammar. We have tried our best to choose books that approach their subjects with the same kind of informative—but still creative—way we have used.

Writing Better—Grammar

The Transitive Vampire: A Handbook of Grammar for the Innocent, the Eager and the Doomed. Karen Elizabeth Gordon, Time Publishing Company. New York, New York (1984).

Modern Business Language and Usage in Dictionary Form. Harold J. Janis. Doubleday and Company. Garden City, New York (1984).

Dictionary of Contemporary Usage, 2d edition. William and Mary Morris. Harper and Row Publishing Company. New York, New York (1985).

Write Right! A Desk Drawer Digest of Punctuation, Grammar and Style. Jan Venolia. Ten Speed Press. Berkeley, California (1982).

Writing Better—Style

Put That in Writing! Jonathan Price. Viking Press. Minneapolis, Minnesota (1984). call number: HF 5718.P74

Writing with Precision: How to Write So That You Cannot Possibly Be Misunderstood. Jefferson D. Bates. Acropolis Books. Washington, D.C. (1980).

How to Write Plain English. Rudolf Flesch. Harper and Row Publishers. New York, New York (1979).

The Elements of Style. William Strunk. MacMillan Books. New York, New York (1959). call number: PE 1408.5772

Resume Writing*

Résumés for Hard Times—How to Make Yourself a Hot Property. Robert Weinstein. Fireside Books. New York, New York (1982). call number: HF5383.P35

Your First Résumé. Ronald W. Fry. The Career Press. Hawthorne, New Jersey (1989). call number: HF5383.F34

The Damn Good Résumé Guide. Yana Parker. Ten Speed Press. Berkeley, California (1989). call number: HF5383.P35

How to Prepare Your Curriculum Vitae. Acy L. Jackson. VGM Career Books. Lincolnwood, Illinois (1993).

Résumés for College Students and Recent Graduates, Professional Resume series. VGM Career Books. Lincolnwood, Illinois (1993).

The Basic Guide to Résumé Writing. Public Library Association Job and Career Information Service Committee. VGM Career Books. Lincolnwood, Illinois (1991).

How to Write a Winning Résumé. Deborah Perlmutter Bloch. VGM Career Books. Lincolnwood, Illinois (1993).

*If you are preparing a resume in a particular field, you may wish to seek out books that direct their format to that industry. See your local library or bookstore for these titles.

Business Letter Format

Handbook for Business Writing. Sue L. Baugh. VGM Career Books. Lincolnwood, Illinois (1993).

Effective Letters in Business. Robert L. Shirter. McGraw Hill Publishing Company. New York, New York (1984).

Webster's Guide to Business Correspondence. John S. Feilden. Prentice Hall. Englewood Cliffs, New Jersey (1984).

The Business Writing Handbook. William C. Paxson. Bantam Books. New York, New York (1984).

How to Write Business Letters. Barron's Educational Series. Woodbury, New York (1982). call number: HF5721.G43

Business Letters the Easy Way. Andrea B. Geffner. Barron's Educational Series. New York, New York (1982).

Letter Perfect: How to Write Business Letters that Work. Ferd Nauheim. Van Nostrand Reinhold. New York, New York (1982).

Interviewing

Help! My Job Interview Is Tomorrow! How to Use the Library to Research an Employer. Mary Ellen Templeton. Neal-Schuman Publishers. New York, New York (1991).

How to Have a Winning Job Interview. Deborah Perlmutter Bloch. VGM Career Books. Lincolnwood, Illinois (1992).

Successful Interviewing for College Seniors. John D. Singleton. VGM Career Books. Lincolnwood, Illinois (1992).

Winning the Job Interview Game—New Strategies for Getting Hired. Bruce R. Hammond. Liberty Hall Press. Blue Ridge Summit, Pennsylvania (1990).

Sweaty Palms: The Neglected Art of Being Interviewed. Anthony H. Medley. Ten Speed Press. Berkeley, California (1984). call number: HF 5549.5M34

Interviews for Success—A Practical Guide to Increasing Job Interviews, Offers and Salaries. Carol Rae Krannich. Impact Publications. Woodbury, Virginia (1990).

Career Directions—Planning and Tactics

What Color Is Your Parachute? Robert Nelson Bolles. Ten Speed Press. Berkeley, California (1994).

Career Planning and Development for College Students and Recent Graduates. John E. Steele. VGM Career Books. Lincolnwood, Illinois (1991).

Occupational Outlook Handbook, 1992–93 edition. VGM Career Books. Lincolnwood, Illinois (1992).

Joyce Lain Kennedy's Career Book. Joyce Lain Kennedy. VGM Career Books. Lincolnwood, Illinois (1992).

The Harvard Guide to Careers. Martha P. Leape. Harvard University Press. Cambridge, Massachusetts (1987).

The Complete Job Search Book. Richard H. Beatty. John Wiley & Sons, Inc. New York, New York (1988). call number: 331.702 L437

Guerilla Tactics in the New Job Market. Thomas Jackson. Bantam Business Books. New York, New York (1991). call number 5382.7J29

General References

The Handbook of Nonsexist Writing. Casey Miller. Lippincott & Growell. New York, New York (1980). call number: PN 218.M5

Arco's Office Guide to Spelling and Word Division. Arco Publishing Company. New York, New York (1984).

VGM CAREER BOOKS

OPPORTUNITIES IN
*Available in both paperback and
  hardbound editions*
Accounting
Acting
Advertising
Aerospace
Agriculture
Airline
Animal and Pet Care
Architecture
Automotive Service
Banking
Beauty Culture
Biological Sciences
Biotechnology
Book Publishing
Broadcasting
Building Construction Trades
Business Communication
Business Management
Cable Television
Carpentry
Chemical Engineering
Chemistry
Child Care
Chiropractic Health Care
Civil Engineering
Cleaning Service
Commercial Art and Graphic Design
Computer Aided Design and
    Computer Aided Mfg.
Computer Maintenance
Computer Science
Counseling & Development
Crafts
Culinary
Customer Service
Dance
Data Processing
Dental Care
Direct Marketing
Drafting
Electrical Trades
Electronic and Electrical Engineering
Electronics
Energy
Engineering
Engineering Technology
Environmental
Eye Care
Fashion
Fast Food
Federal Government
Film
Financial
Fire Protection Services
Fitness
Food Services
Foreign Language
Forestry
Gerontology
Government Service
Graphic Communications
Health and Medical
High Tech
Home Economics
Hospital Administration
Hotel & Motel Management
Human Resources Management
  Careers
Information Systems
Insurance
Interior Design
International Business
Journalism
Laser Technology
Law

Law Enforcement and Criminal Justice
Library and Information Science
Machine Trades
Magazine Publishing
Management
Marine & Maritime
Marketing
Materials Science
Mechanical Engineering
Medical Technology
Metalworking
Microelectronics
Military
Modeling
Music
Newspaper Publishing
Nursing
Nutrition
Occupational Therapy
Office Occupations
Opticianry
Optometry
Packaging Science
Paralegal Careers
Paramedical Careers
Part-time & Summer Jobs
Performing Arts
Petroleum
Pharmacy
Photography
Physical Therapy
Physician
Plastics
Plumbing & Pipe Fitting
Podiatric Medicine
Postal Service
Printing
Property Management
Psychiatry
Psychology
Public Health
Public Relations
Purchasing
Real Estate
Recreation and Leisure
Refrigeration and Air Conditioning
Religious Service
Restaurant
Retailing
Robotics
Sales
Sales & Marketing
Secretarial
Securities
Social Science
Social Work
Speech-Language Pathology
Sports & Athletics
Sports Medicine
State and Local Government
Teaching
Technical Communications
Telecommunications
Television and Video
Theatrical Design & Production
Transportation
Travel
Trucking
Veterinary Medicine
Visual Arts
Vocational and Technical
Warehousing
Waste Management
Welding
Word Processing
Writing
Your Own Service Business

CAREERS IN Accounting; Advertising;
Business; Communications; Computers;
Education; Engineering; Health Care;
High Tech; Law; Marketing; Medicine;
Science

CAREER DIRECTORIES
Careers Encyclopedia
Dictionary of Occupational Titles
Occupational Outlook Handbook

CAREER PLANNING
Admissions Guide to Selective
  Business Schools
Career Planning and Development for
  College Students and Recent
  Graduates
Careers Checklists
Careers for Animal Lovers
Careers for Bookworms
Careers for Culture Lovers
Careers for Foreign Language
  Aficionados
Careers for Good Samaritans
Careers for Gourmets
Careers for Nature Lovers
Careers for Numbers Crunchers
Careers for Sports Nuts
Careers for Travel Buffs
Guide to Basic Resume Writing
Handbook of Business and
  Management Careers
Handbook of Health Care Careers
Handbook of Scientific and
  Technical Careers
How to Change Your Career
How to Choose the Right Career
How to Get and Keep
  Your First Job
How to Get into the Right Law School
How to Get People to Do Things
  Your Way
How to Have a Winning Job Interview
How to Land a Better Job
How to Make the Right Career Moves
How to Market Your College Degree
How to Prepare a *Curriculum Vitae*
How to Prepare for College
How to Run Your Own Home Business
How to Succeed in Collge
How to Succeed in High School
How to Write a Winning Resume
Joyce Lain Kennedy's Career Book
Planning Your Career of Tomorrow
Planning Your College Education
Planning Your Military Career
Planning Your Young Child's
  Education
Resumes for Advertising Careers
Resumes for College Students & Recent
  Graduates
Resumes for Communications Careers
Resumes for Education Careers
Resumes for High School Graduates
Resumes for High Tech Careers
Resumes for Sales and Marketing Careers
Successful Interviewing for College
  Seniors

SURVIVAL GUIDES
Dropping Out or Hanging In
High School Survival Guide
College Survival Guide

VGM Career Horizons
a division of *NTC Publishing Group*
4255 West Touhy Avenue
Lincolnwood, Illinois 60646-1975